POP ANTHOLOGY - BOOK 2
50 POP SONGS FOR ALL PIANO METHODS

ISBN 978-1-5400-1546-4

HAL•LEONARD®

Visit Hal Leonard Online at
www.halleonard.com

Contact us:
Hal Leonard
7777 West Bluemound Road
Milwaukee, WI 53213
Email: info@halleonard.com

In Europe, contact:
Hal Leonard Europe Limited
42 Wigmore Street
Marylebone, London, W1U 2RN
Email: info@halleonardeurope.com

In Australia, contact:
Hal Leonard Australia Pty. Ltd.
4 Lentara Court
Cheltenham, Victoria, 3192 Australia
Email: info@halleonard.com.au

Be Our Guest

from BEAUTY AND THE BEAST

Music by Alan Menken
Lyrics by Howard Ashman
Arranged by Fred Kern

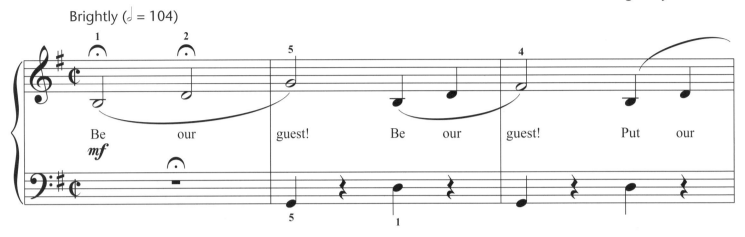

Be our guest! Be our guest! Put our

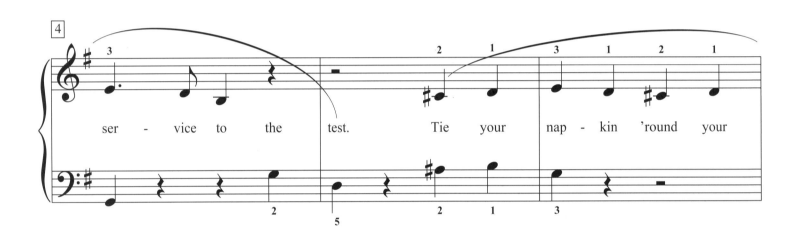

ser - vice to the test. Tie your nap - kin 'round your

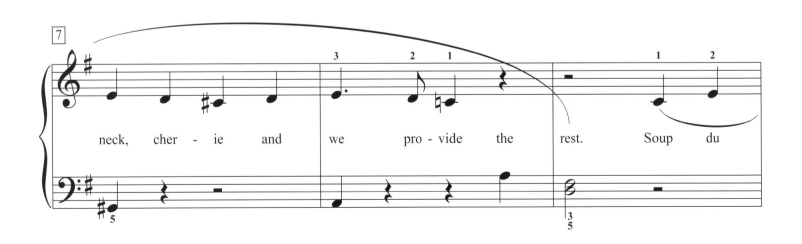

neck, cher - ie and we pro - vide the rest. Soup du

jour! Hot hors d'oeuvres! Why, we on - ly live to

serve Try the grey stuff, it's de - li - cious! Don't be -

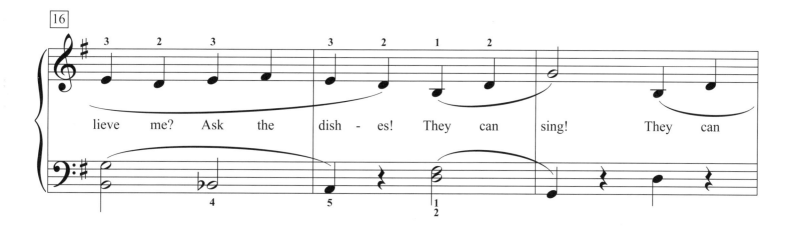

lieve me? Ask the dish - es! They can sing! They can

dance! Af - ter all, Miss, this is France! And a

5

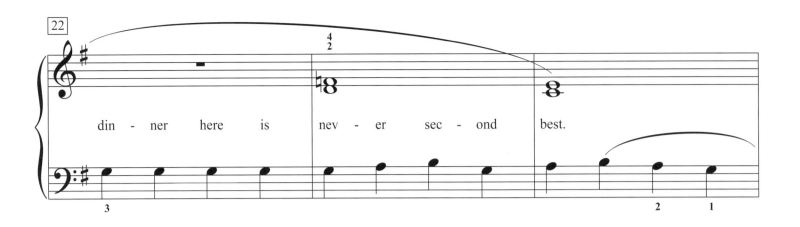

din - ner here is nev - er sec - ond best.

Go on, un - fold your men - u, take a

glance, and then ____ you'll be our guest, be our

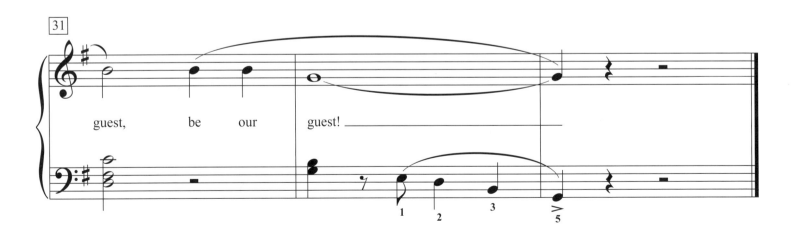

guest, be our guest! ____

Candle in the Wind

Words and Music by ELTON JOHN
and BERNIE TAUPIN
Arranged by Carol Klose

Gently (♩ = 88)

With pedal

Good-bye, Nor - ma Jean.
Lone - li - ness was tough,

Though I nev - er
the tough-est role

knew you at all,
you ev - er played.

you had the grace to
Hol - ly - wood cre - at - ed a

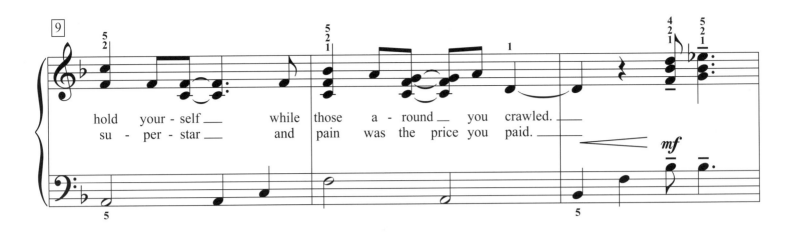

hold your-self ___ while those a-round ___ you crawled. ___
su - per - star ___ and pain was the price you paid. ___

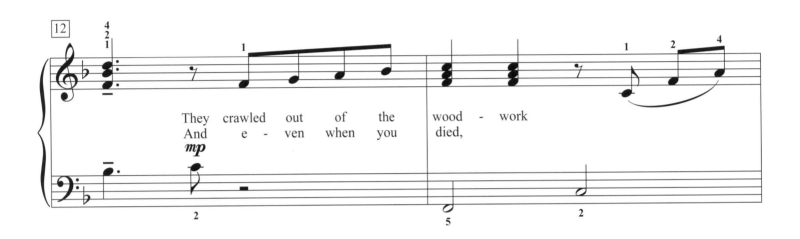

They crawled out of the wood - work
And e - ven when you died,

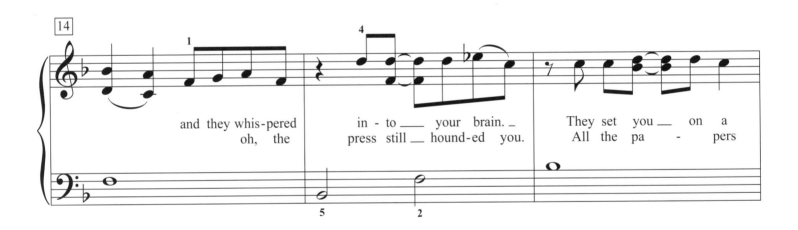

and they whis-pered
oh, the

in - to ___ your brain. ___
press still ___ hound-ed you.

They set you ___ on a
All the pa - pers

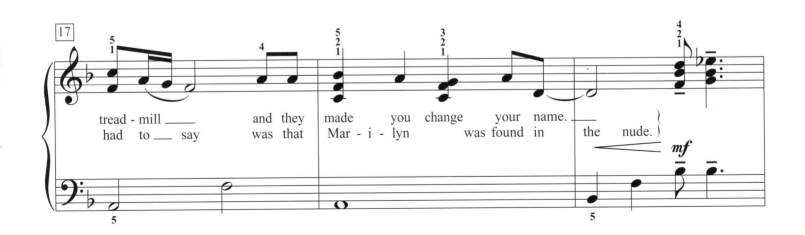

tread - mill ___ and they made you change your name. ___
had to ___ say was that Mar - i - lyn was found in the nude.

It seems to me _____ you lived your life _____ like a

can - dle in _____ the wind, _____ nev - er know - ing _____ who to

cling to when the rain set in. _____

would have liked to have known you but I was just a kid. Your

can - dle burned ___ out long be - fore ___ your

leg - end ev - er did. ___

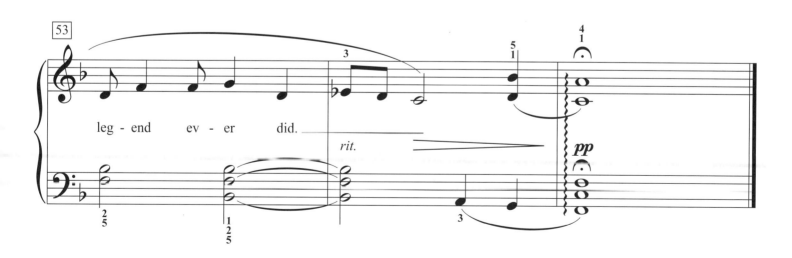

City of Stars

from LA LA LAND

Music by Justin Hurwitz
Lyrics by Benj Pasek & Justin Paul
Arranged by Lynda Lybeck-Robinson

knows? I felt it from the first em - brace I shared with

you that now our dreams may fi - n'lly come

true. Cit - y of stars, —

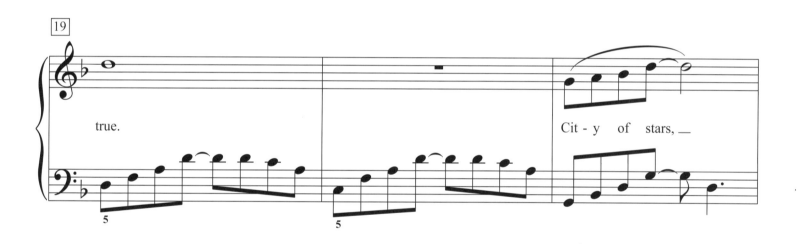

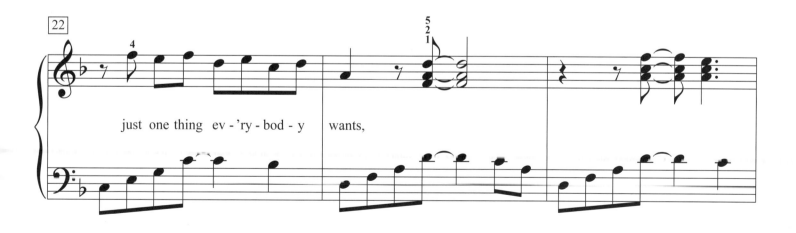

just one thing ev - 'ry - bod - y wants,

there in the bars ___ and through the smoke-screen of the crowd - ed res - tau - rants: ___

___ it's love. Yes, all we're look-ing for ___ is

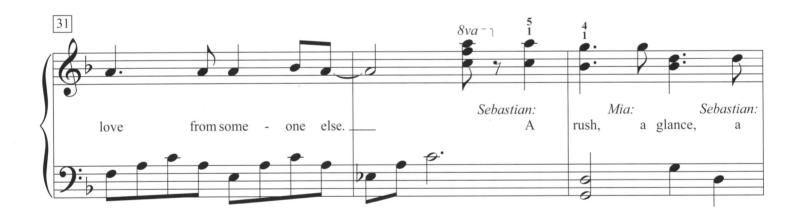

love from some - one else. ___

Sebastian:
A rush, a glance, a

Mia:
rush,

Sebastian:
a glance, a

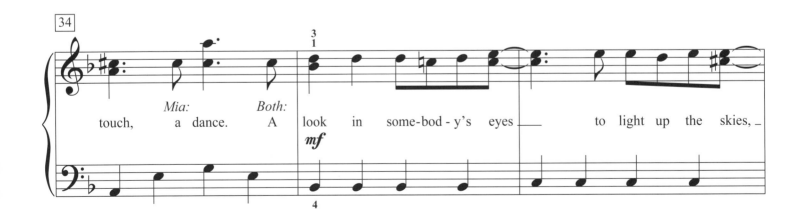

Mia:
touch, a dance.

Both:
A look in some-bod - y's eyes ___ to light up the skies, ___

mf

14

to o-pen the world __ and send it reel-ing. A voice that says, "I'll be here, _

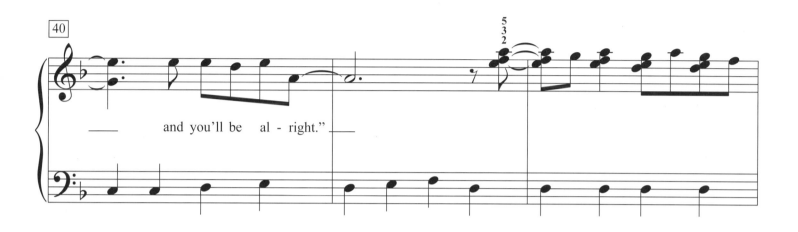

_ and you'll be al-right." _

I don't care if I know __ just where I will go, __ 'cause all that I need's _

_ this cra-zy feel-ing, a rat-tat-tat on my heart... _

15

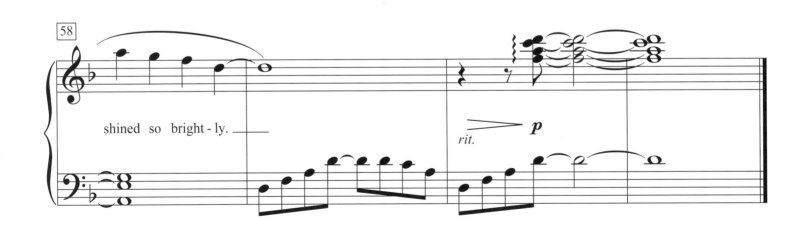

Dancing Queen

Words and Music by Benny Andersson,
Björn Ulvaeus and Stig Anderson
Arranged by Carol Klose

Steady Rock beat (♩ = 100)

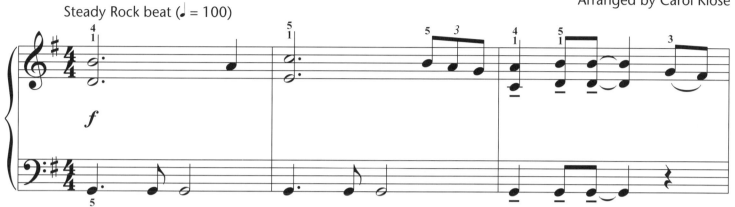

You can dance. You can jive,

17

hav - ing the time of your life. _____ Oh, _____ see that girl. _

cresc.

Watch that scene, _ dig - gin' the danc - ing queen. _

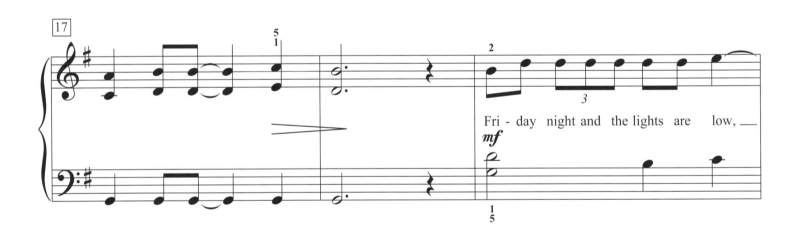

Fri - day night and the lights are low, _

mf

_____ look - ing out for a place to go, _____ oh, _____

where they play the right mu - sic. Get-ting in the swing, you come to look for a king.

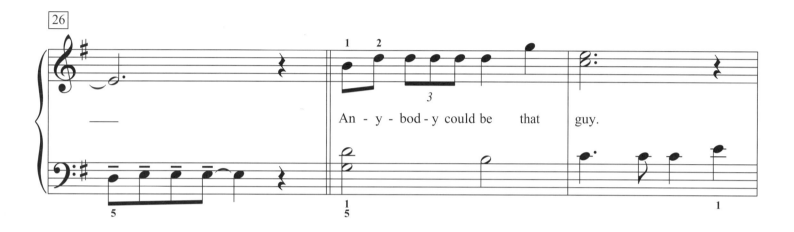

An - y - bod - y could be that guy.

Night is young and the mu - sic's high. With a bit of rock mu - sic,

ev - 'ry-thing is fine. You're in the mood for a dance, _ and when you

get the chance, _____ you are the danc - ing queen, _

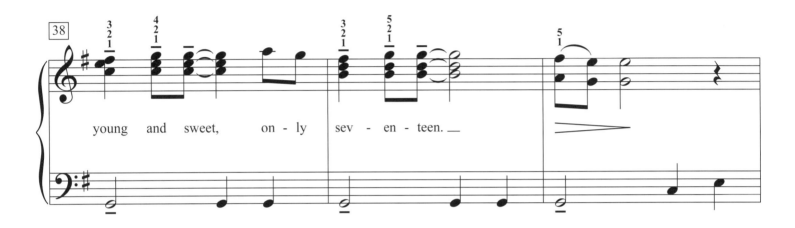

young and sweet, on - ly sev - en - teen. _

Danc - ing queen, _ feel the beat _ from the tam - bou - rine. _____

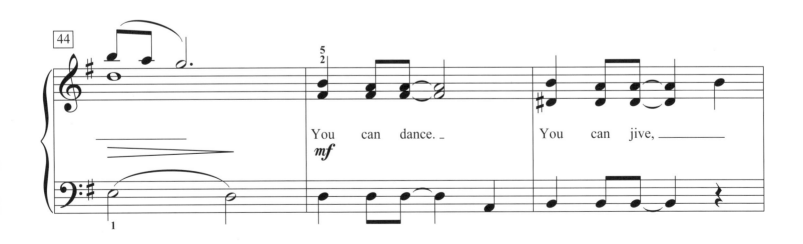

You can dance. _ You can jive, _____

hav - ing the time of your life. _____ Oh, _____ see that girl. _

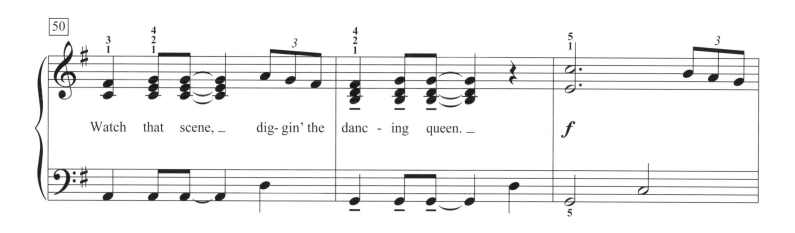

Watch that scene, _ dig- gin' the danc - ing queen. _

Dig- gin' the danc - ing queen. _

Dancing Through Life

from the Broadway Musical WICKED

Music and Lyrics by
Stephen Schwartz
Arranged by Carol Klose

With expression (♩ = 88)

The trou-ble with schools is they al-ways try to teach the wrong les - son.

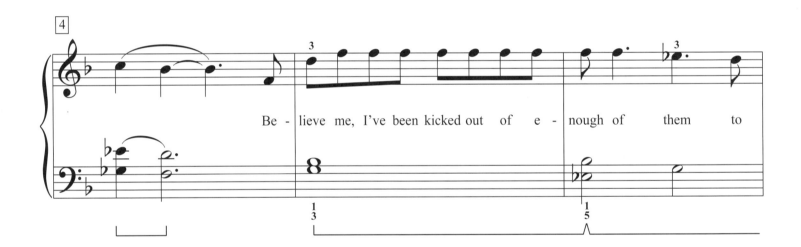

Be - lieve me, I've been kicked out of e - nough of them to

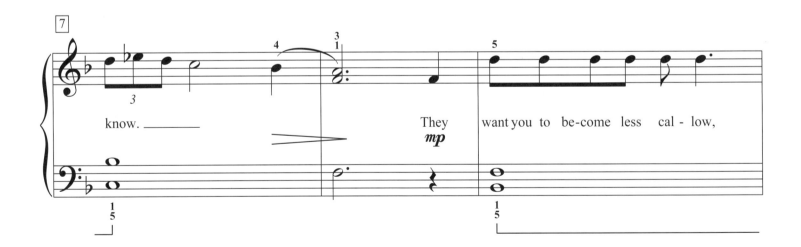

know. _____ They want you to be-come less cal - low,

less shal - low, but I say, "Why in - vite stress in?

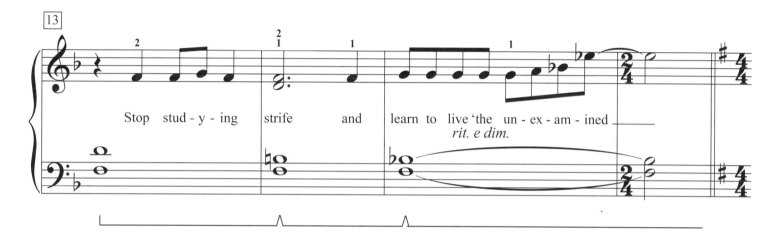

Stop stud - y - ing strife and learn to live 'the un - ex - am - ined
rit. e dim.

Pop "Dance beat" (♩ = 116)

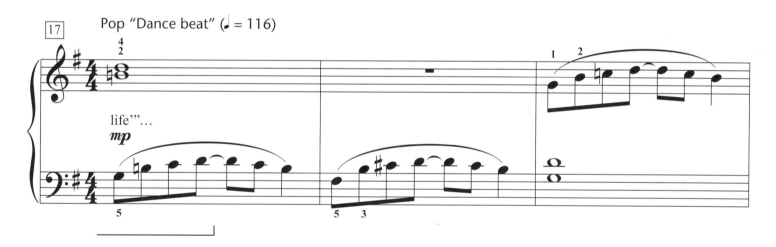

life'"...
mp

Danc - ing through life, __ skim - ming the sur - face,
Danc - ing through life, __ sway - ing and sweep - ing,
mf

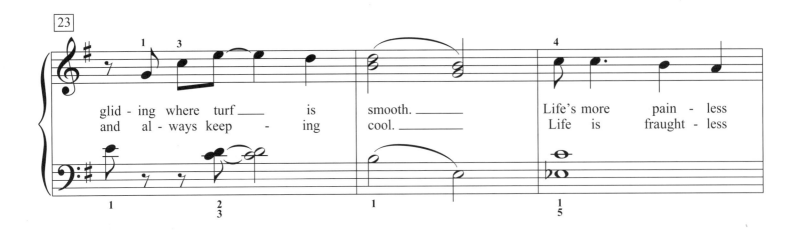

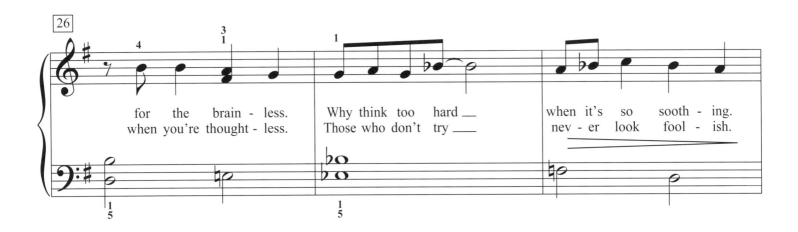

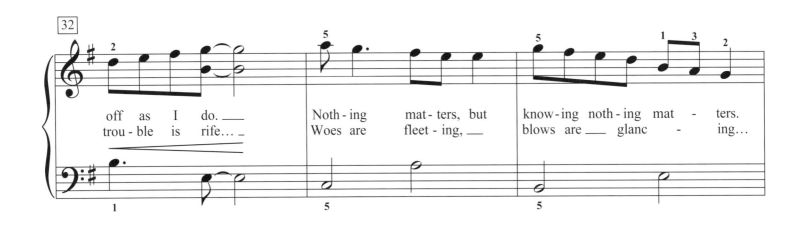

It's just life   so keep danc - ing   through...

It's just life   so keep danc - ing   through.

The Entertainer

(A Ragtime Two-Step)

By Scott Joplin
(1868-1917)
Arranged by Carol Klose

Not fast (♩ = 126-138)

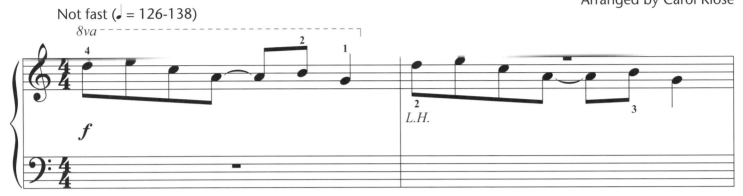

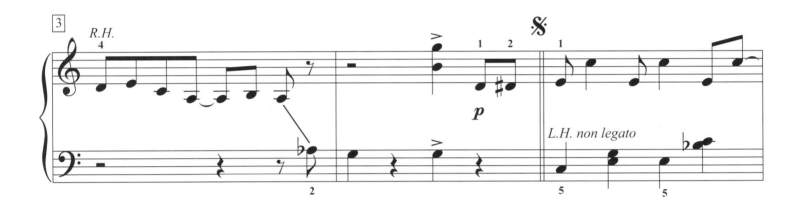

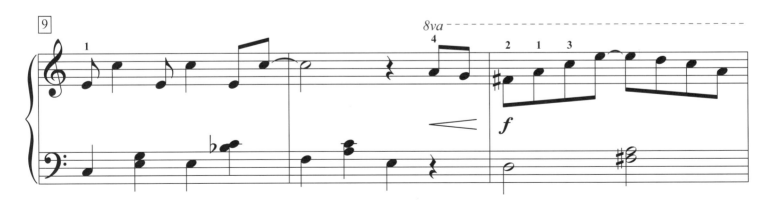

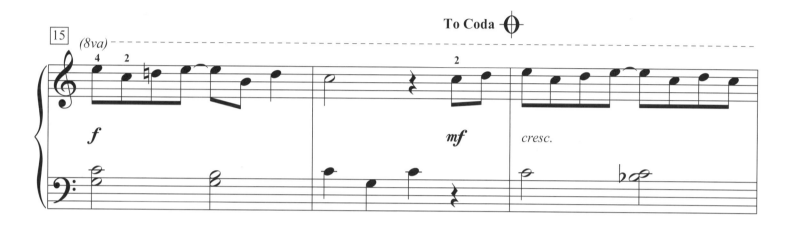

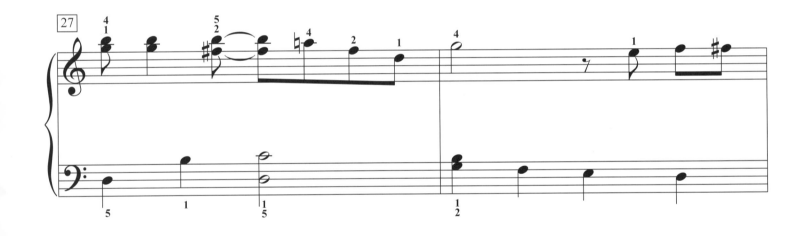

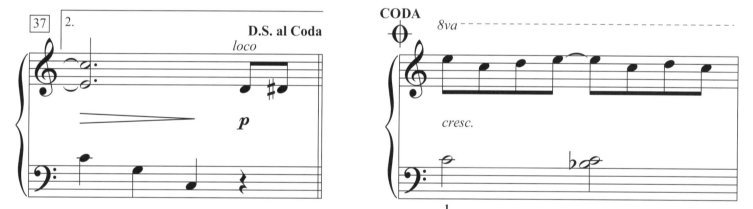

Friend Like Me

from ALADDIN

Music by Alan Menken
Lyrics by Howard Ashman
Arranged by Mona Rejino

Well, A - li Ba - ba had them for - ty thieves. Sche - her - a - za - de had a thou - sand tales. _

But, mas - ter, you in luck, 'cause up your sleeves __ you got a

brand of mag - ic nev - er fails. You got some pow - er in your

cor - ner now, some heav - y am - mu - ni - tion in your camp. __

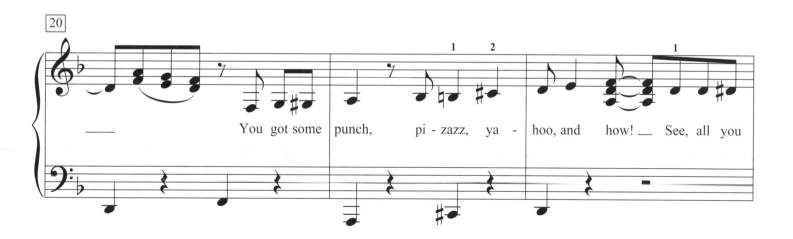

__ You got some punch, pi - zazz, ya - hoo, and how! __ See, all you

gotta do is rub that lamp. And I'll __ say Mis - ter A -

lad - din sir, __ what will your pleas - ure be? Let me

take your or - der, jot it down. You ain't nev - er had a friend like

me. No, no, no. Life is your res - tau - rant __ and

I'm your mai - tre d'. _____ C' - mon, whis - per what it

is you want. You ain't nev - er had a friend like me. Yes, sir, we

pride our - selves on ser - vice. You're the boss, the king, the

shah. Say what you wish. It's yours! True dish, how 'bout a

lit - tle more bak - la - va? _____ *mf* Have some of

col - umn "A." ___ Try all of col - umn "B." I'm

in the mood _ to help you, dude. You ain't nev - er had a friend, nev - er

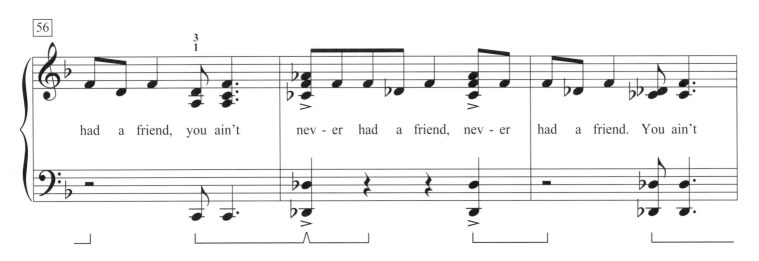

had a friend, you ain't nev - er had a friend, nev - er had a friend. You ain't

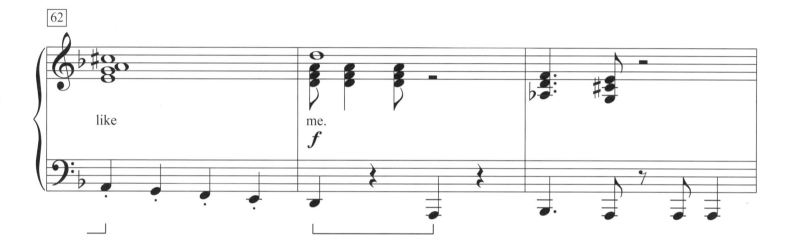

Happy

from DESPICABLE ME 2

Words and Music by
Pharrell Williams
Arranged by Lynda Lybeck-Robinson

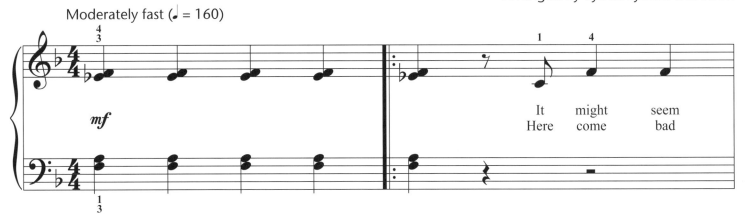

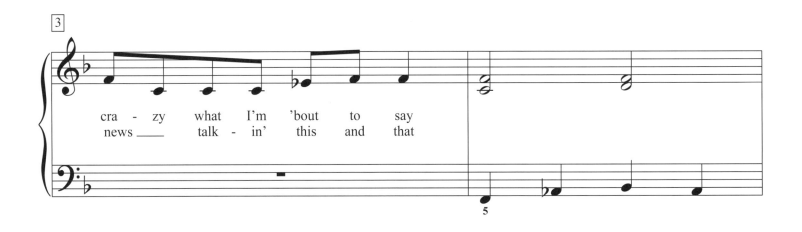

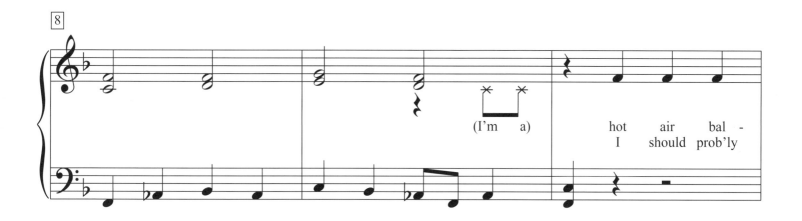

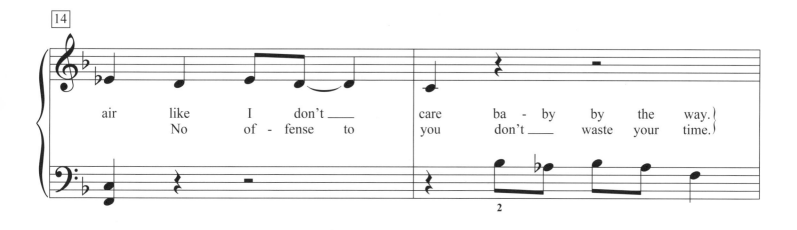

if you feel like that's what you wan - na do.

mf

Bring me down, ___ can't noth - in' Bring me down; ___

___ your love is too high. Bring me down ___ can't noth - in'

Bring me down. (Let me tell you now.) Bring me down, _

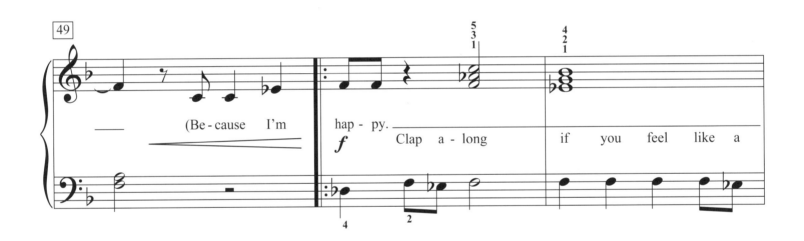

if you feel ___ like hap - pi - ness is the truth.

Be - cause I'm

hap - py. ___

Clap a - long ___ if you know what hap - pi - ness is to you.

Be - cause I'm hap - py.) ___

Clap a - long if you feel like

that's what you wan - na do.

(Be - cause I'm

Fields of Gold

Music and Lyrics by Sting
Arranged by Phillip Keveren

So she took her love ___ for to gaze a - while ___ up -
You'll re - mem-ber me ___ when the west wind moves ___ up -

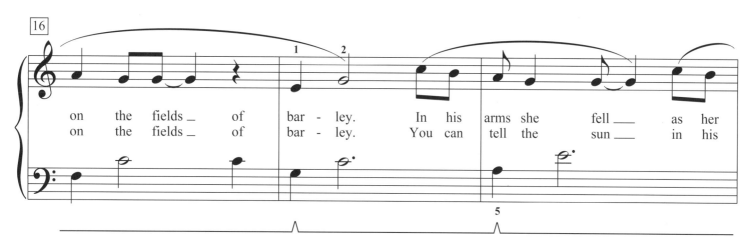

on the fields ___ of bar - ley. In his arms she fell ___ as her
on the fields ___ of bar - ley. You can tell the sun ___ in his

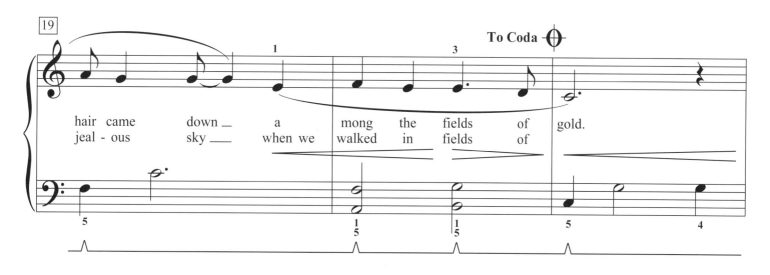

To Coda ⊕

hair came down ___ a - mong the fields of gold.
jeal - ous sky ___ when we walked in fields of

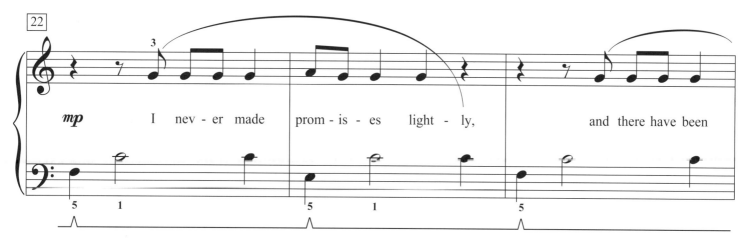

mp I nev - er made prom - is - es light - ly, and there have been

43

some that I've bro - ken, but I swear in the days still left we'll

walk in fields of gold.

a tempo   *pp*   Man - y

CODA

gold,   when we walked in fields of gold.
molto rit.

Heart and Soul
from the Paramount Short Subject A SONG IS BORN

Words by Frank Loesser
Music by Hoagy Carmichael
Arranged by Phillip Keveren

I beg to be a - dored. Lost con - trol and tum-bled o - ver-board,

glad - ly, that mag - ic night we kissed there in the

moon - mist. Oh! but your lips were thrill - ing, much too

thrill - ing. Nev - er be - fore were mine so strange - ly

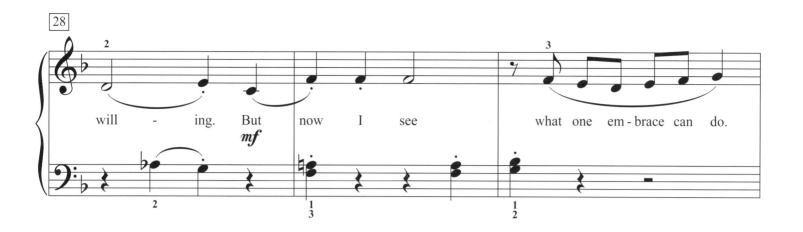

will - ing. But now I see what one em-brace can do.

Look at me, it's got me lov - ing you mad - ly,

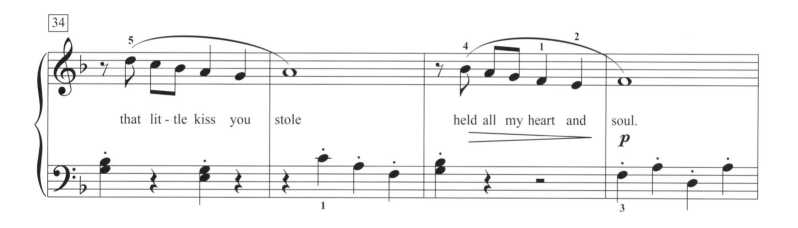

that lit - tle kiss you stole held all my heart and soul.

He's a Pirate

from PIRATES OF THE CARIBBEAN: THE CURSE OF THE BLACK PEARL

Music by Klaus Badelt,
Geoffrey Zanelli and Hans Zimmer
Arranged by Jennifer Linn

I'm a Believer

Words and Music by
Neil Diamond
Arranged by Mona Rejino

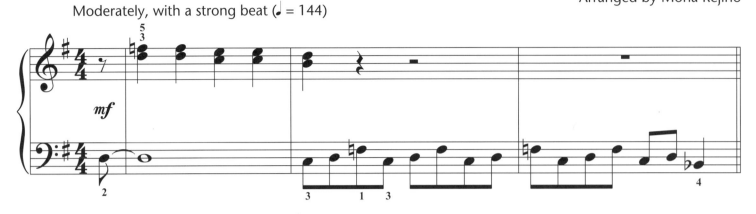

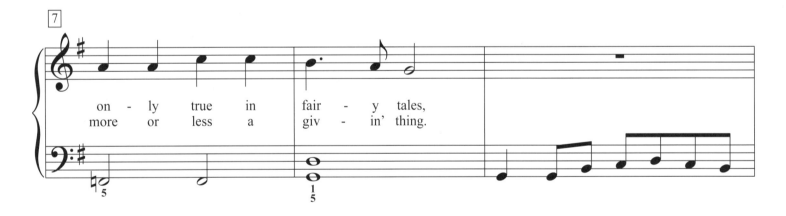

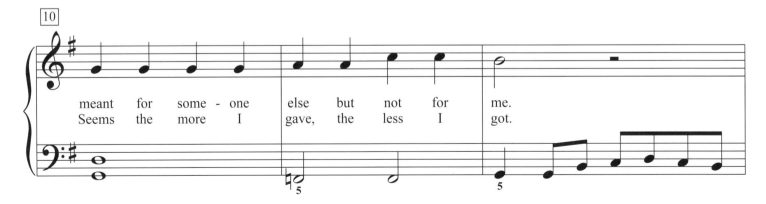

mind. I'm in love.

I'm a be - liev - er. I could-n't leave ____ her if I

tried.

mf

dim. e rit.

mp

I Will Always Love You

Words and Music by
Dolly Parton
Arranged by Mona Rejino

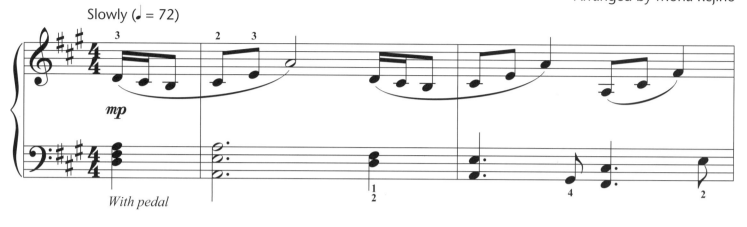

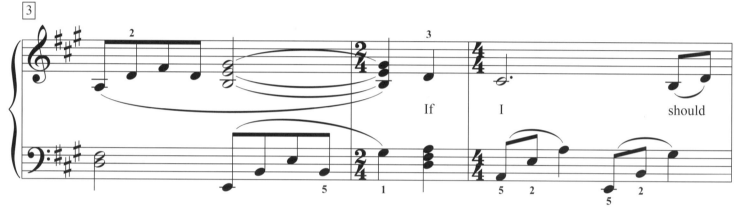

way. _____ And I _____ will al - ways _ love _

you. _____ I _____ will al - ways _ love _ you.

Bit - ter - sweet mem - o - ries, that's all

I am tak - ing with me. _____ Good - bye, please don't

I Will Remember You

Theme from THE BROTHERS McMULLEN

Words and Music by Sarah McLachlan,
Seamus Egan and Dave Merenda
Arranged by Fred Kern

Moderately slow (♩ = 80)

(Play both hands 8va on repeat.)

I will re-mem-ber you. Will you re-mem-ber

me? Don't let your life ___ pass ___ you by. ___

___ Weep not for ___ the mem-o-ries. ___

Kiss the Girl
from THE LITTLE MERMAID

Music by Alan Menken
Lyrics by Howard Ashman
Arranged by Phillip Keveren

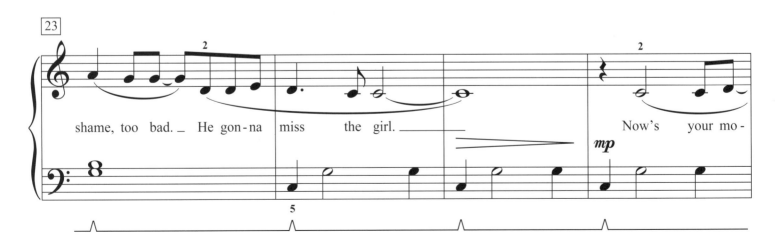

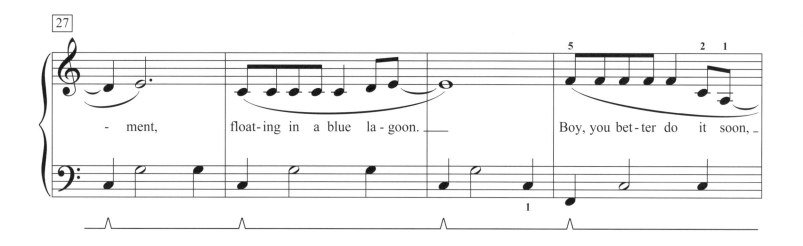

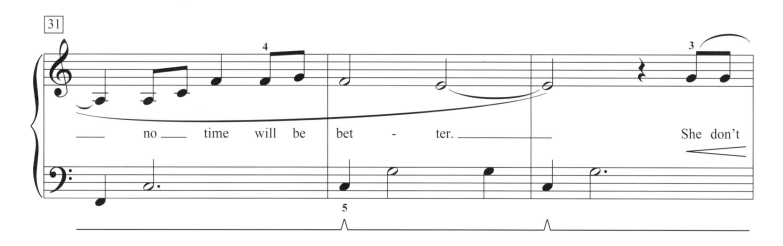

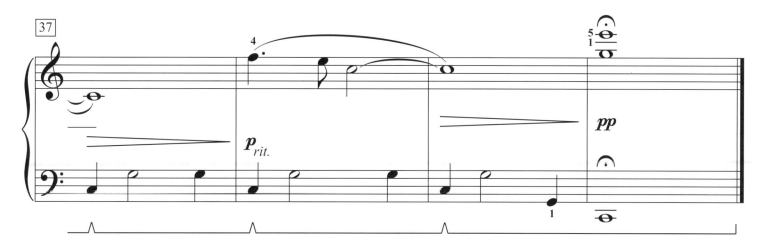

Let It Be

Words and Music by John Lennon
and Paul McCartney
Arranged by Mona Rejino

When I find my-self___ in times of trou-ble
when the bro-ken-heart-ed peo-ple

Moth-er Mar-y comes to me speak-ing words of wis-
liv-ing in the world a-gree there will be an an-

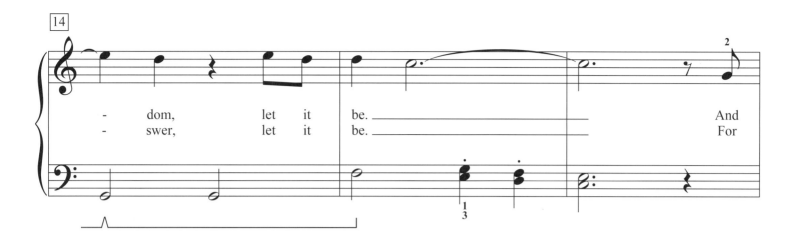

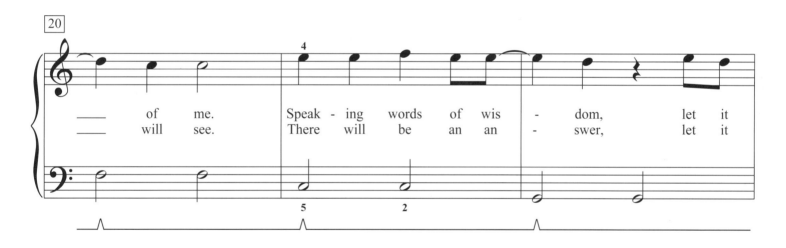

Memory

from CATS

Music by Andrew Lloyd Webber
Text by Trevor Nunn after T.S. Eliot
Arranged by Phillip Keveren

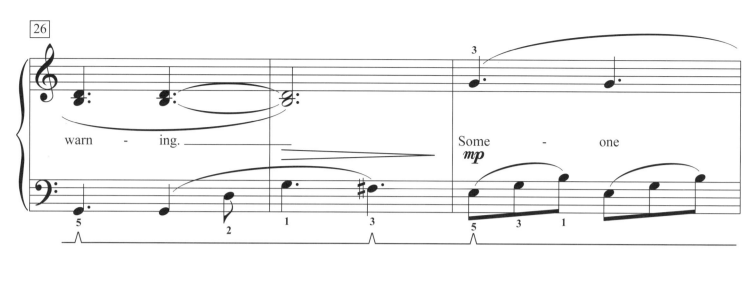

warn - ing. _____ Some - one
mp

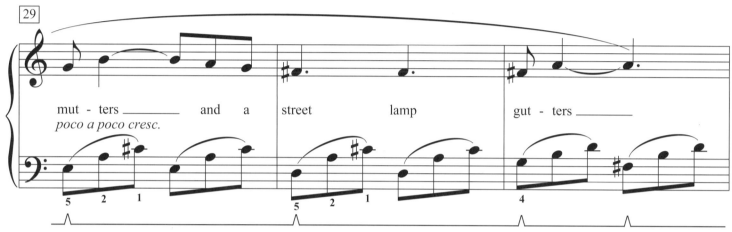

mut - ters _____ and a street lamp gut - ters _____
poco a poco cresc.

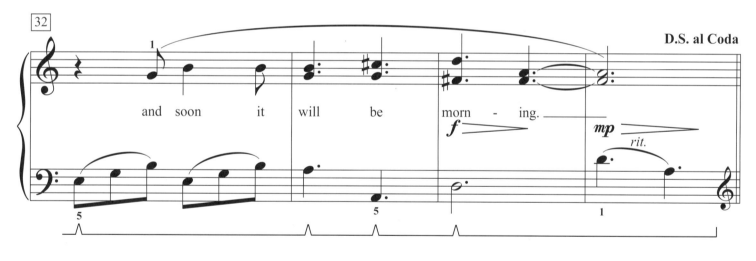

D.S. al Coda

and soon it will be morn - ing. _____
f *mp*
rit.

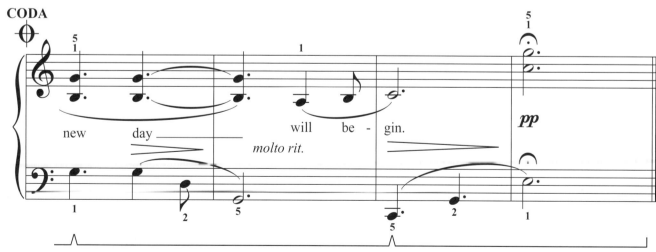

CODA

new day _____ will be - gin.
molto rit.
pp

71

The Phantom of the Opera

from THE PHANTOM OF THE OPERA

Music by Andrew Lloyd Webber
Lyrics by Charles Hart
Additional Lyrics by Richard Stilgoe and Mike Batt
Arranged by Fred Kern

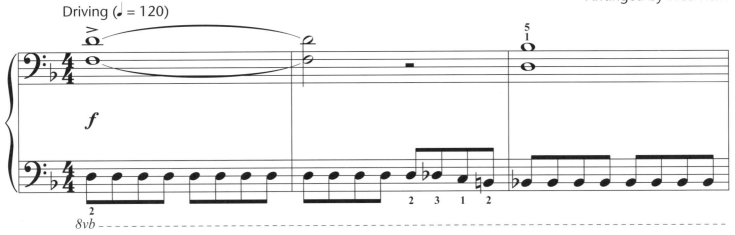

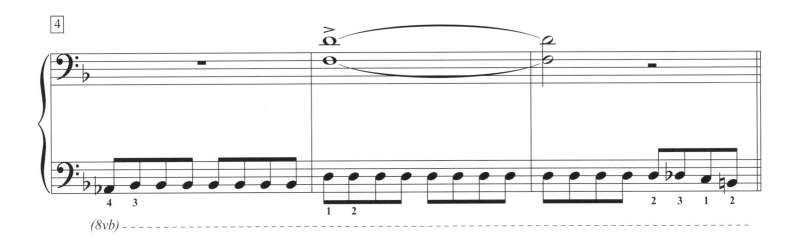

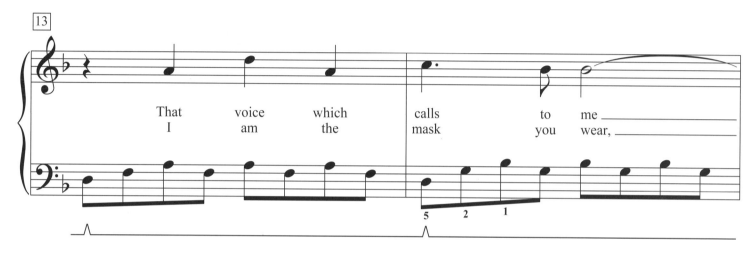

Ob-La-Di, Ob-La-Da

Words and Music by John Lennon
and Paul McCartney
Arranged by Eugénie Rocherolle

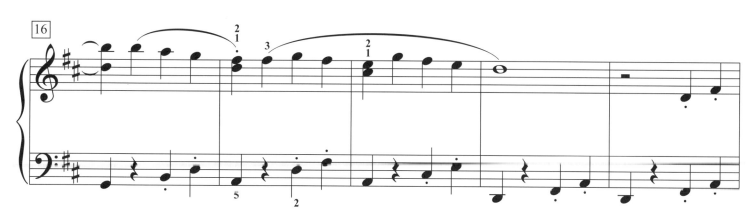

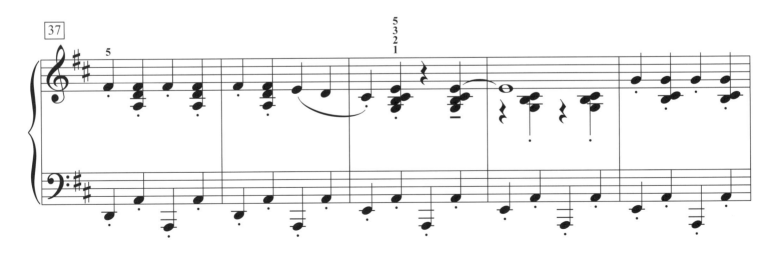

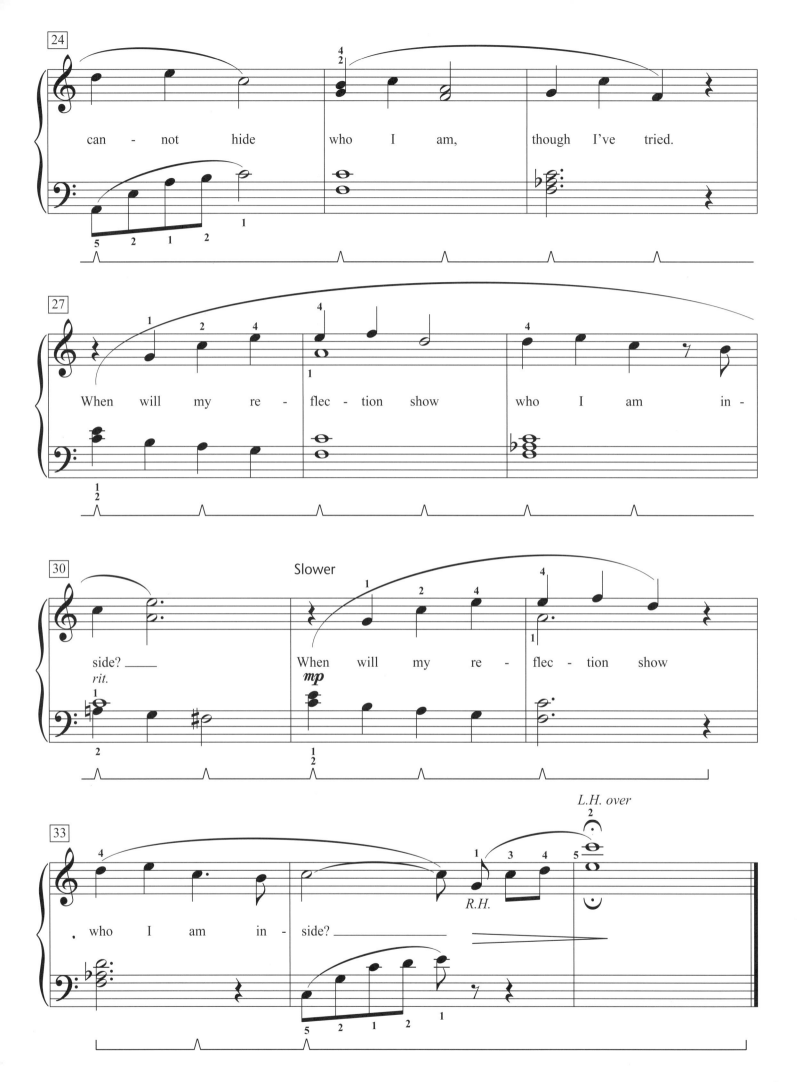

can - not hide   who I am,   though I've tried.

When will my re - flec - tion show   who I am in -

side? ___   When will my re - flec - tion show
rit.   *mp*

. who I am in - side? ___

82

Star Wars Medley

Music by John Williams
Arranged by Jennifer & Mike Watts

The Imperial March (Darth Vader's Theme)
from STAR WARS: THE EMPIRE STRIKES BACK

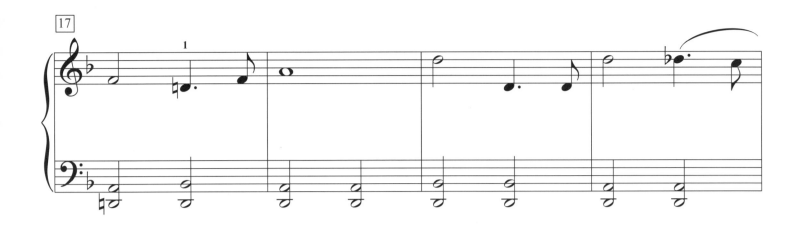

L'istesso (♩ = 92)
Cantina Band
from STAR WARS: A NEW HOPE

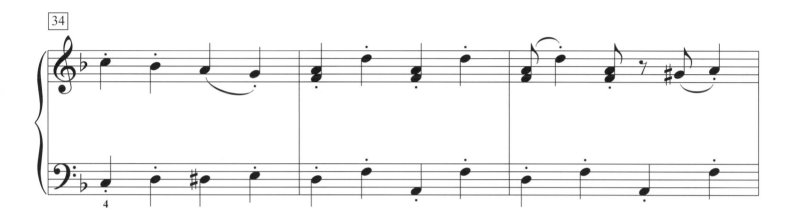

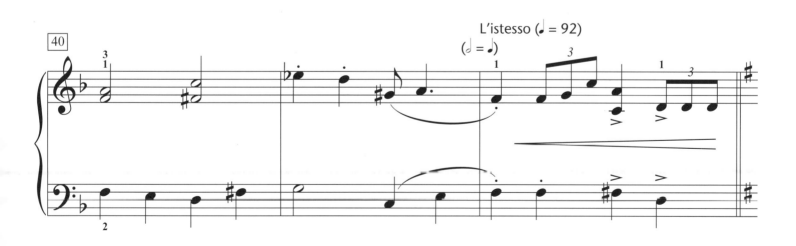

Star Wars (Main Theme)
from STAR WARS: A NEW HOPE

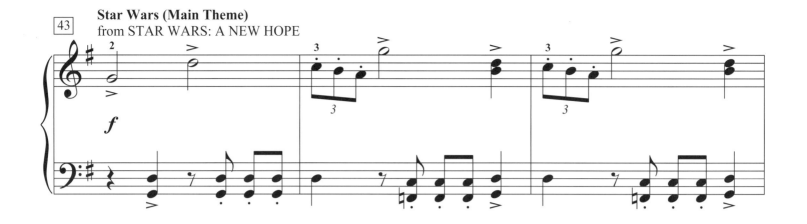

Unchained Melody

Lyric by Hy Zaret
Music by Alex North
Arranged by Fred Kern

A Whole New World

from ALADDIN

Music by Alan Menken
Lyrics by Tim Rice
Arranged by Mona Rejino

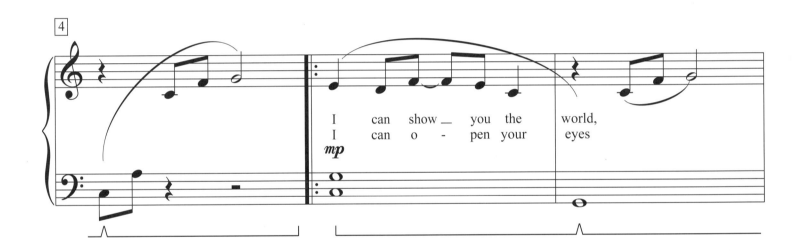

I can show __ you the world,
I can o - pen your eyes

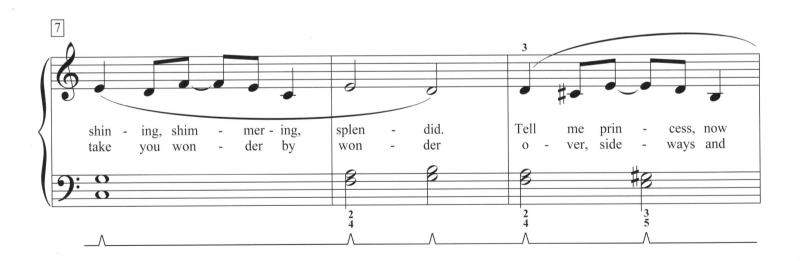

shin - ing, shim - mer - ing, splen - did. Tell me prin - cess, now
take you won - der by won - der o - ver, side - ways and

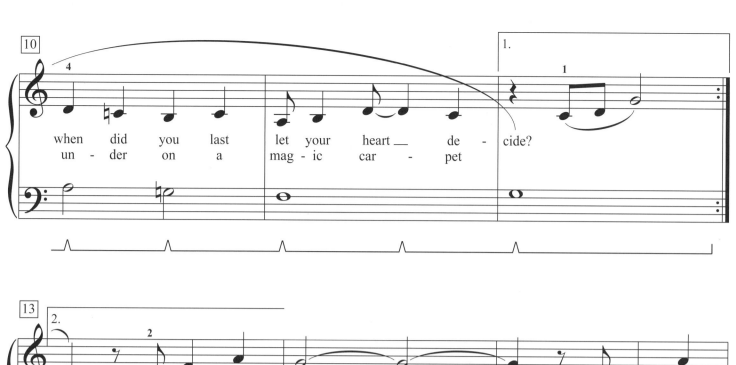

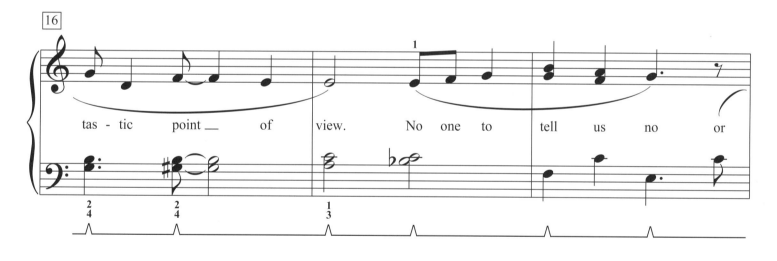

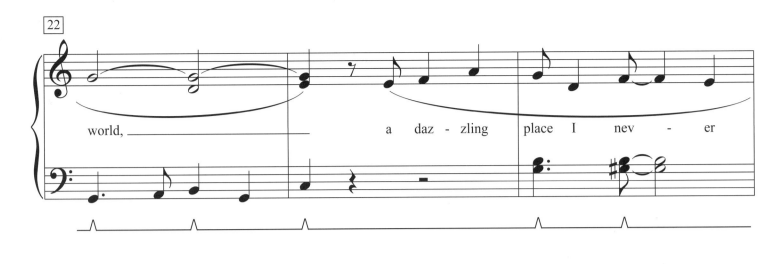

world, _____ a daz - zling place I nev - er

knew. But when I'm way up here it's

crys - tal clear that now I'm in a whole new world with

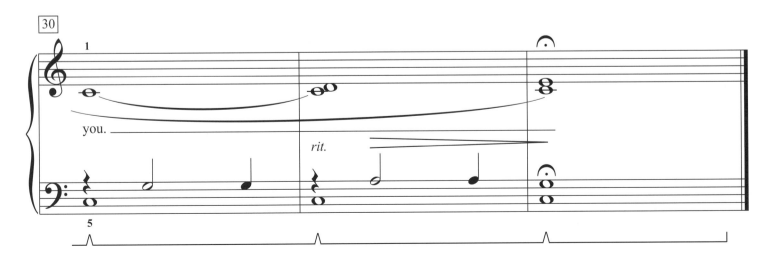

you. _____

rit.

You'll Never Walk Alone

from CAROUSEL

Lyrics by Oscar Hammerstein II
Music by Richard Rodgers
Arranged by Carol Klose

Slowly, with reverence (♩ = 104-112)

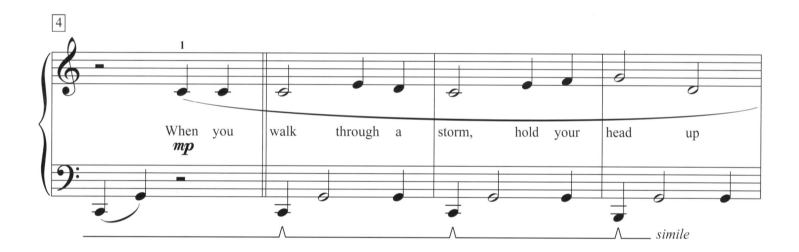

When you walk through a storm, hold your head up high and don't be a-fraid of the dark.

At the end of the storm is a gold - en

sky and the sweet sil - ver song of a lark.

Walk on through the wind, walk on through the

simile

rain, though your dreams be tossed and

INTERMEDIATE

Accidentally in Love

from the Motion Picture SHREK 2

Words and Music by Adam F. Duritz,
Dan Vickrey, David Immergluck,
Matthew Malley and David Bryson
Arranged by Carol Klose

Come on, come on, move a lit-tle clos - er. Come on, come on, I

want to hear you whis - per. Come on, come on, set - tle down in - side __ my

love. __ Ah. __ Come on, come on,

jump a lit - tle high - er. Come on, come on, if you feel a lit - tle light - er.

Come on, come on, we were once up - on a time __ in __ love. __

All I Ask of You
from THE PHANTOM OF THE OPERA

Music by Andrew Lloyd Webber
Lyrics by Charles Hart
Additional Lyrics by Richard Stilgoe
Arranged by Mona Rejino

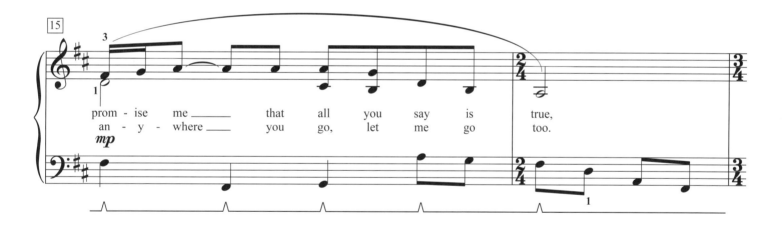

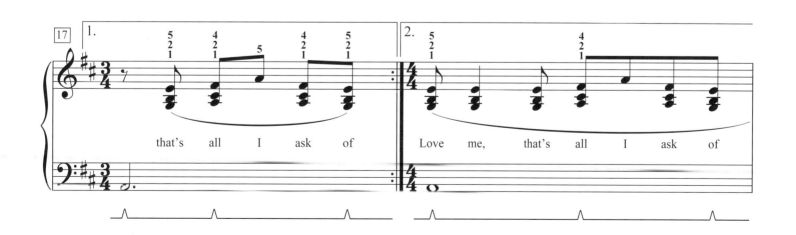

An - y - where you go, let me go

too; love me, that's all I ask of you.

104

Always on My Mind

Words and Music by Wayne Thompson,
Mark James and Johnny Christopher
Arranged by Mona Rejino

Slow and steady (♩ = 69)

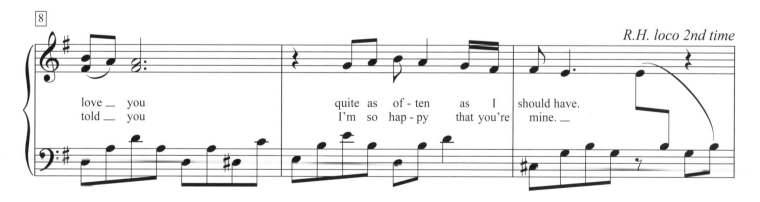

Lit - tle things I should have said and done, ___
If I made you feel ___ sec - ond best, ___

I just nev - er took the time. ___
I'm so sor - ry, I was blind. ___

You were al - ways on my mind;
cresc.
mf

To Coda ⊕

you were al - ways on my ___ mind.
mp
1.
mp
2.
mind.

D.S. al Coda

Baby Elephant Walk

from the Paramount Picture HATARI!

Words by Hal David
Music by Henry Mancini
Arranged by Mona Rejino

Bless the Beasts and Children

from BLESS THE BEASTS AND CHILDREN

Words and Music by Barry DeVorzon
and Perry Botkin, Jr.
Arranged by Fred Kern

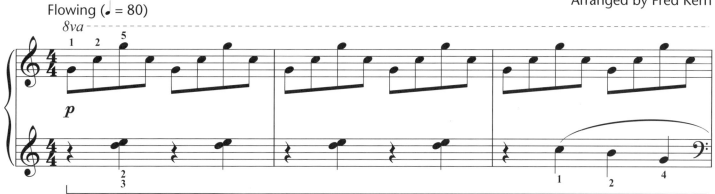

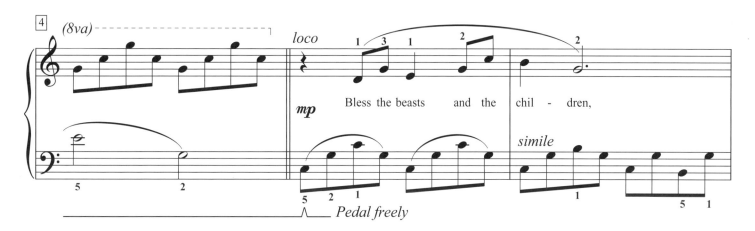

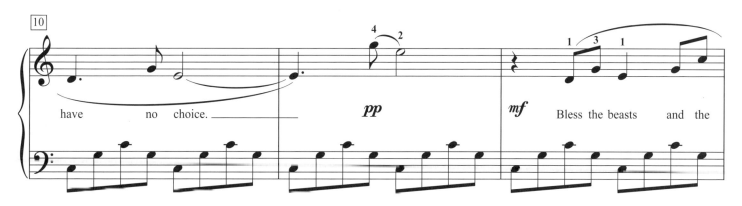

chil - dren,
for the world
can nev - er be

the world they see.

Light their way
when the dark - ness
sur -

rounds them.
Give them love,
let it

shine
all a - round
them.

Bless the beasts and the chil - dren, give them shel - ter

from a storm. _____ Keep them safe,

keep them warm.

keep them warm. _____

Colors of the Wind

from POCAHONTAS

Music by Alan Menken
Lyrics by Stephen Schwartz
Arranged by Mona Rejino

Moderately, with expression (♩ = 80)

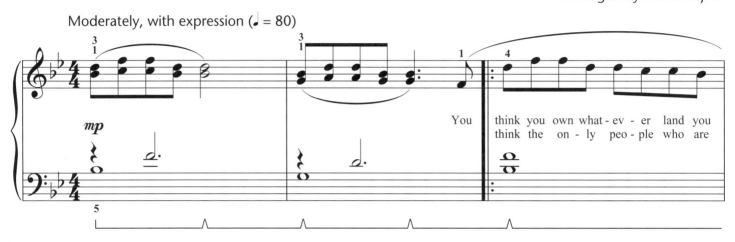

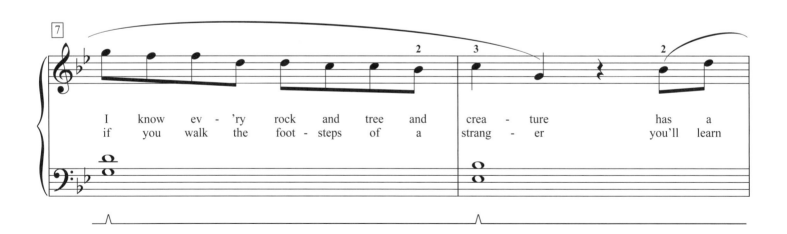

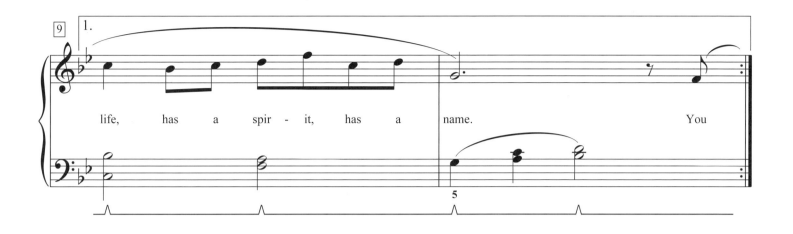

life, has a spir - it, has a name. You

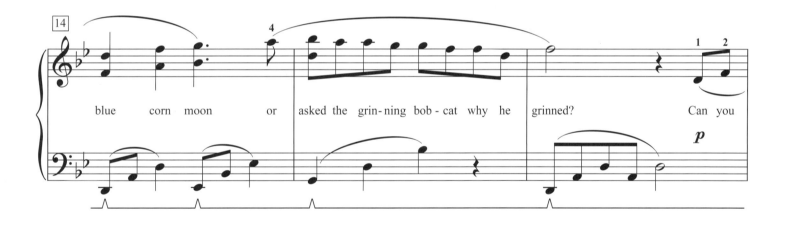

things you nev - er knew you nev - er knew. Have you ev - er heard the wolf cry to the

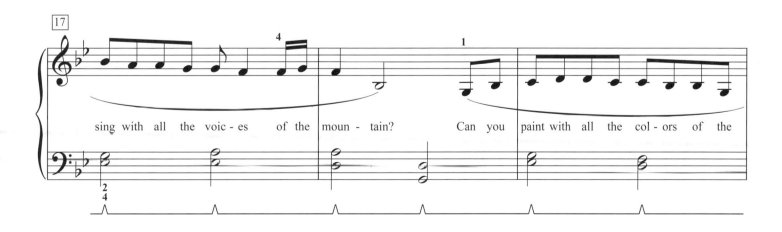

blue corn moon or asked the grin-ning bob - cat why he grinned? Can you

sing with all the voic - es of the moun - tain? Can you paint with all the col - ors of the

wind? Can you paint with all the col - ors of the

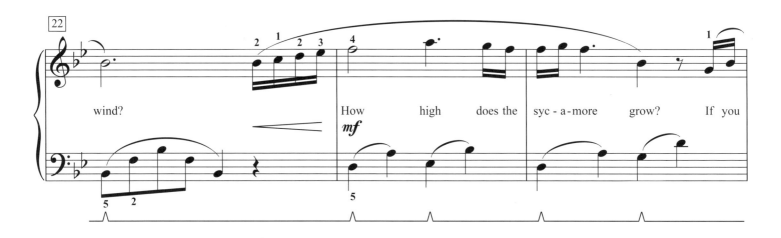

wind? How high does the syc - a - more grow? If you

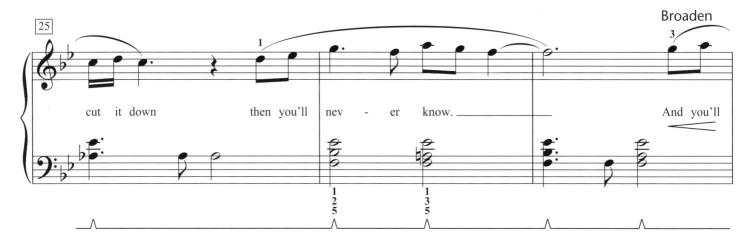

Broaden

cut it down then you'll nev - er know. _____ And you'll

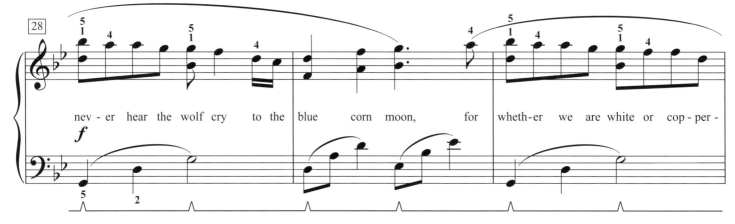

nev - er hear the wolf cry to the blue corn moon, for wheth - er we are white or cop - per -

skinned,   we need to sing with all the voic - es   of the moun - tain,   we need to

paint with all the col - ors of the   wind.   You can   own the earth _ and still   all you'll

own is earth un - til   you can paint with all the col - ors of the   wind.

rit.   *a tempo*

p

rit.   *R.H.*

Cruella De Vil

from 101 DALMATIANS

Words and Music by
Mel Leven
Arranged by Carol Klose

ice of her stare; __ all in - no - cent chil - dren had bet - ter be - ware. __ She's

like a spi - der wait - ing for the kill. Look out for Cru - el - la De

cresc.

Vil. At first you think Cru - el - la is a dev - il. But

mf

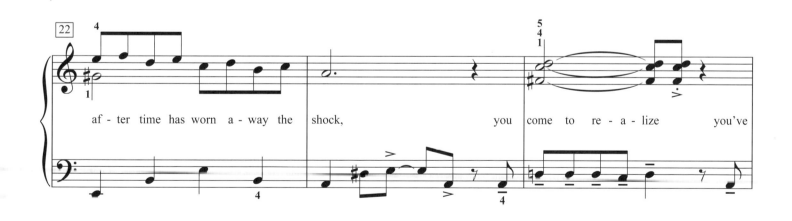

af - ter time has worn a - way the shock, you come to re - a - lize you've

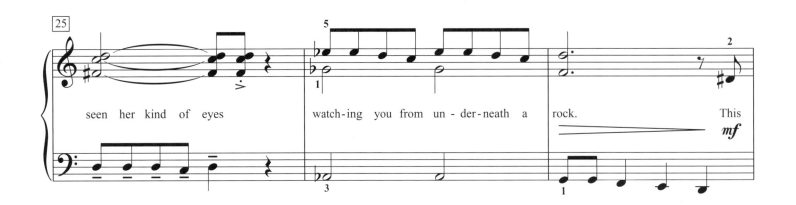

seen her kind of eyes   watch-ing you from un - der - neath a   rock.   This

vam - pire __ bat, __   this in - hu - man beast, _   she ought to be locked up   and

nev - er re - leased.   The world was such a whole-some place un - til   Cru -

cresc.   *f*

el - la,   Cru - el - la   De Vil.

Don't Stop Believin'

Words and Music by Steve Perry,
Neal Schon and Jonathan Cain
Arranged by Jennifer Linn

Moderately fast (♩ = 120)

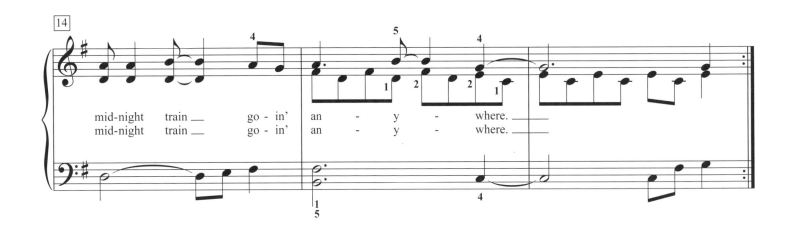

mid-night train __ go - in' an - y - where.
mid-night train __ go - in' an - y - where.

A sing - er in a smok - y room. __

122

The smell of wine and cheap per - fume. _____ For a smile _ they can

share the night. _ It goes on and on _____ and on _____ and on. _____

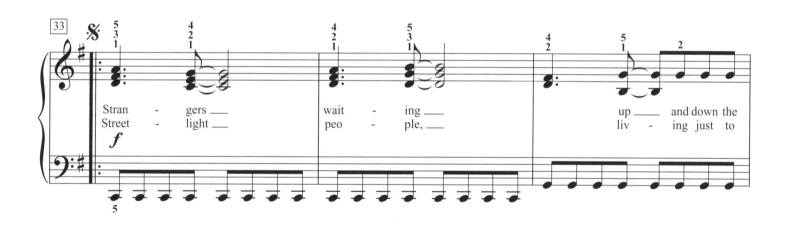

Stran - gers _____ wait - ing _____ up _____ and down the
Street - light _____ peo - ple, _____ liv - ing just to

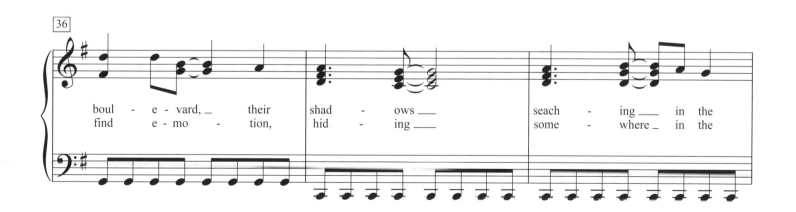

boul - e - vard, _ their shad - ows _____ seach - ing _ in the
find e - mo - tion, hid - ing _____ some - where _ in the

on   and on   and on   and on.   Don't   stop   be-

liev - in'.   Hold on to the   feel - in', _____

street - light   peo - ple. ___

125

From a Distance

Words and Music by Julie Gold
Arranged by Fred Kern

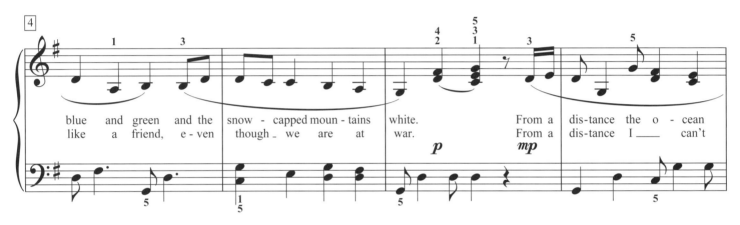

To Coda ⊕

voice of hope ___ it's the | voice of peace, ___ it's the | voice of ev - 'ry ___ man. | God is
hope of hopes, ___ it's the | love of love, ___ it's the | heart of ev - 'ry ___

p *mf*

watch-ing us, | God ___ is watch-ing us, | God ___ is watch-ing us from a | dis - tance ___ God is

p *mf*

D.S. al Coda

watch-ing us, | God ___ is watch-ing us, | God ___ is watch-ing us from a | dis - tance ___ From a

p *mp*

CODA ⊕

man. *p* *mf* *mp*

8vb

127

Hero

Words and Music by Mariah Carey
and Walter Afanasieff
Arranged by Phillip Keveren

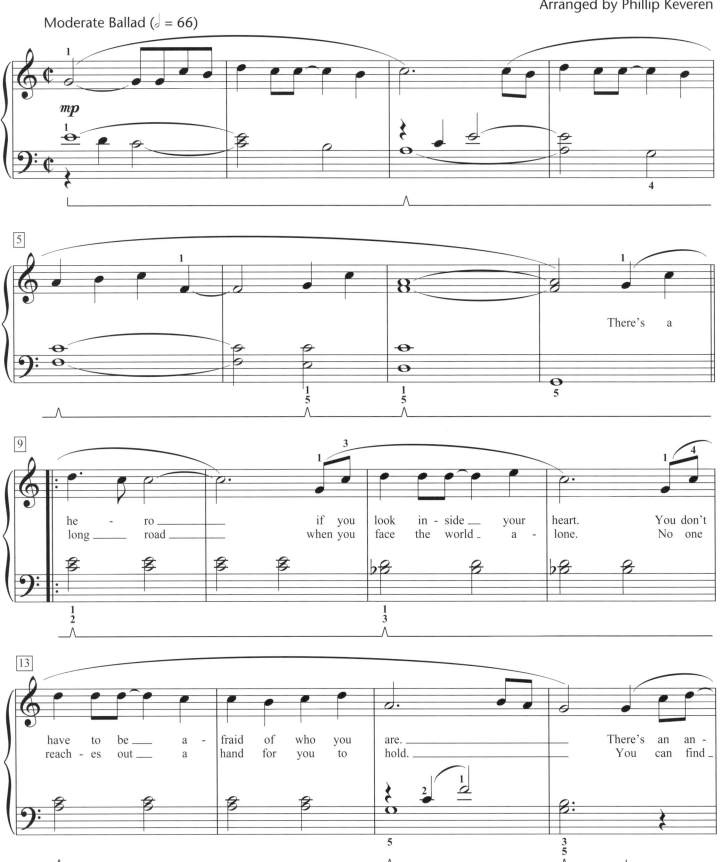

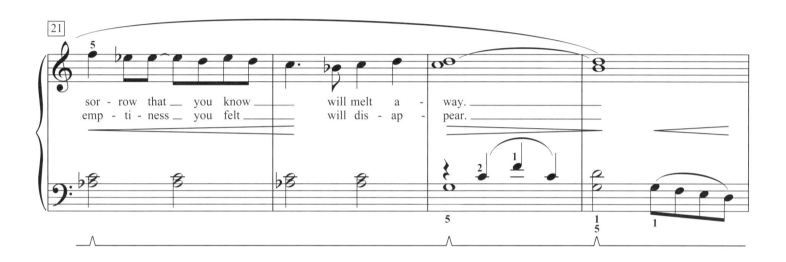

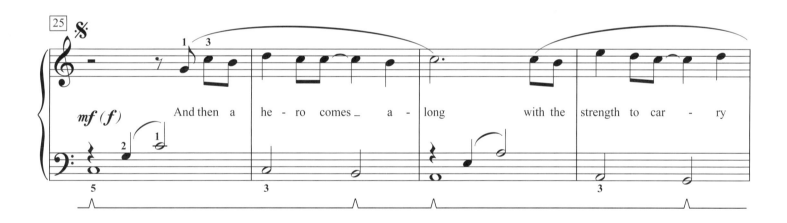

I Dreamed a Dream

from LES MISÉRABLES

Music by Claude-Michel Schönberg
Lyrics by Alain Boublil,
Jean-Marc Natel and Herbert Kretzmer
Arranged by Fred Kern

132

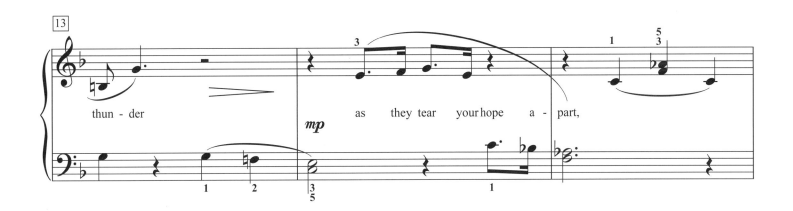

thun - der   as   they   tear   your hope   a - part,

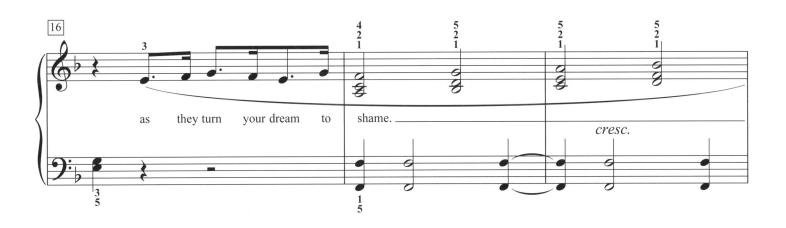

as   they turn   your dream   to   shame.

He slept a sum - mer by my   side.

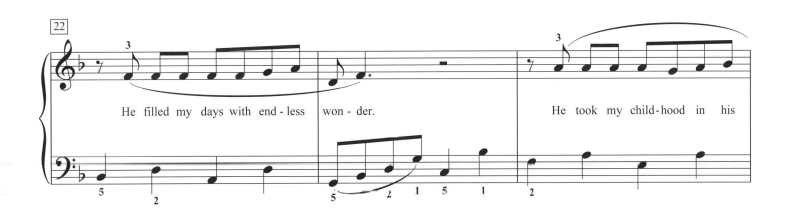

He   filled my days with end - less   won - der.   He took my child-hood in his

stride,

but he was gone when au - tumn came.

mp And still I dream he'll come to me,

that we would live the years to - geth - er.

mf But these are dreams that could not

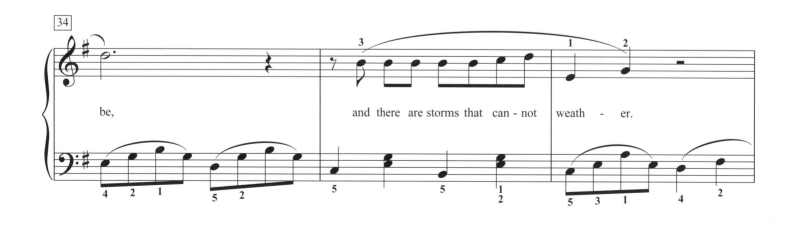

be,

and there are storms that can - not weath - er.

Imagine

Words and Music by
John Lennon
Arranged by Mona Rejino

Slowly (♩ = 76)

I-mag-ine there's no heav-en. _____ It's eas-y if you try. _____

No hell ____ be-low us, _____ a-bove us on-ly

simile

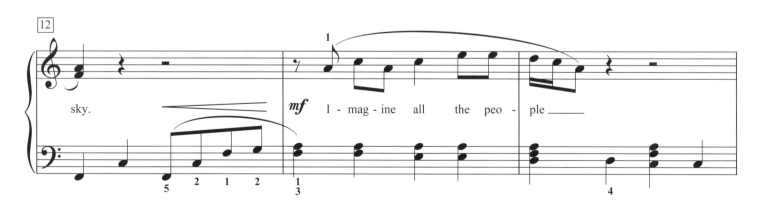

sky. _____ I-mag-ine all the peo-ple _____

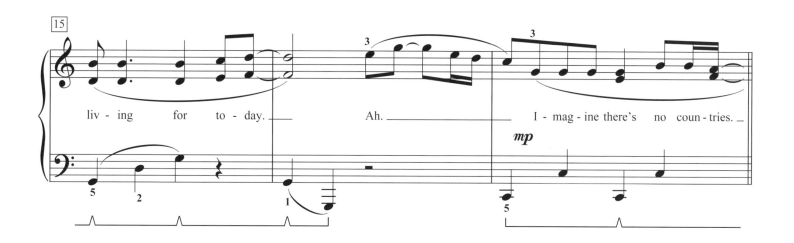

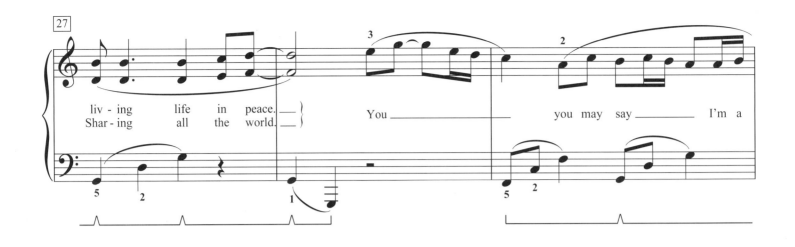

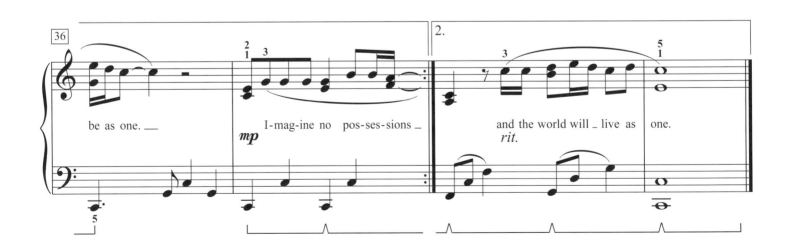

Theme from "Jurassic Park"

from the Universal Motion Picture JURASSIC PARK

Composed by John Williams
Arranged by Mona Rejino

Lean on Me

Words and Music by
Bill Withers
Arranged by Jennifer Linn

But, if we are wise, we know that there's al - ways to -

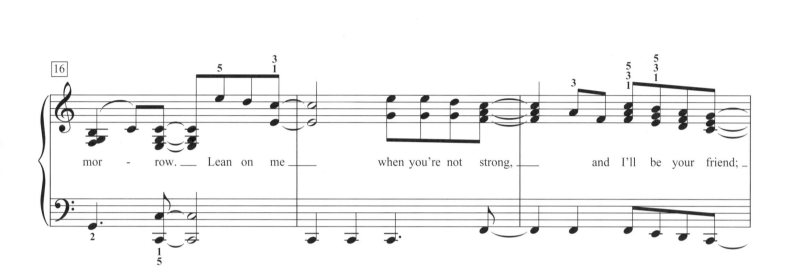

mor - row. Lean on me when you're not strong, and I'll be your friend;

I'll help you car - ry on, for it won't be long

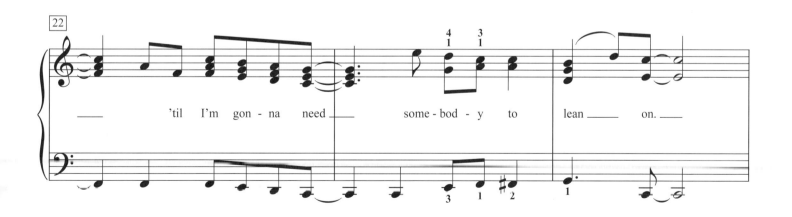

'til I'm gon - na need some - bod - y to lean on.

Please ___ swal-low your pride ___ if I have things ___ you need to bor-
If ___ there is a load ___ you have to bear ___ that you can't car-

-row, ___ for no one can fill ___ those of your needs ___
-ry, ___ I'm right up the road. ___ I'll share your load ___

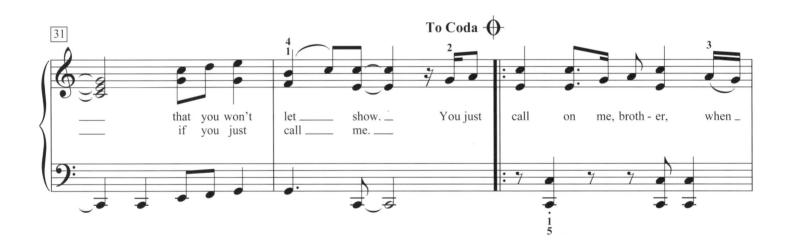

To Coda ⊕

that you won't let ___ show. ___ You just call on me, broth-er, when ___
if you just call ___ me. ___

you need a hand. ___ We all ___ need some-bod-y to lean ___

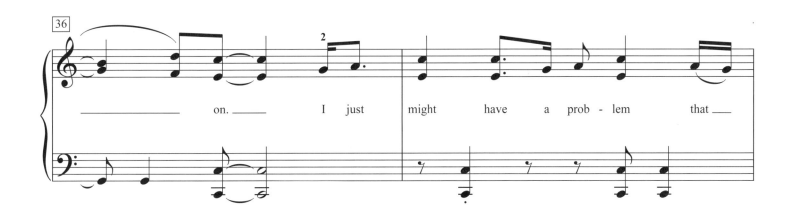

on. _____ I just might have a prob - lem that _____

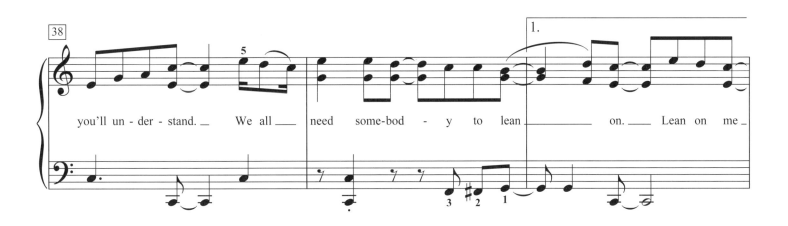

you'll un - der - stand. ___ We all ___ need some-bod - y to lean _____ on. ___ Lean on me ___

_____ when you're not strong ___ and I'll be your friend; ___ I'll help you

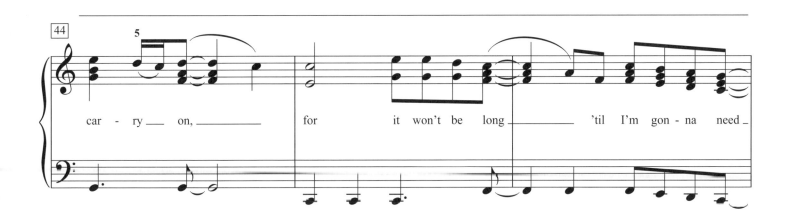

car - ry ___ on, _____ for it won't be long ___ 'til I'm gon - na need ___

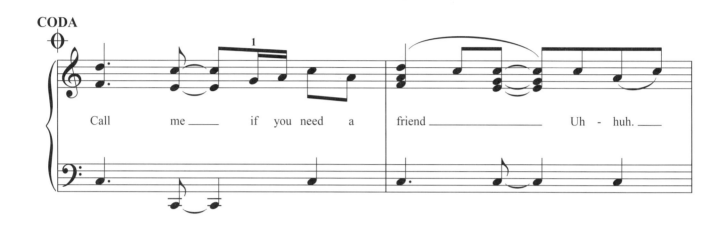

Let It Go
from FROZEN

Music and Lyrics by Kristen Anderson-Lopez
and Robert Lopez
Arranged by Jennifer Linn

Half-time feel, mysterious (♩ = 69)

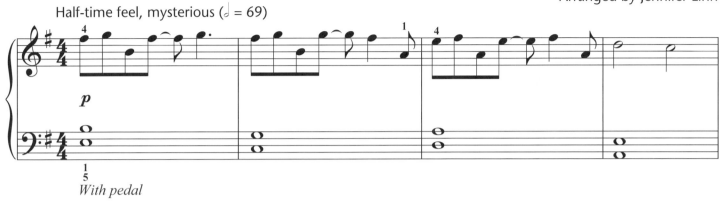

looks like I'm the queen. The wind is howl-

-ing like this swirl - ing storm in - side. Could-n't keep it in,

heav-en knows I tried. *mf* Don't let them in,

don't let them see; be the good girl you al - ways have to

be. Con - ceal, don't feel, don't let them know... *cresc.*

149

The cold nev-er both-ered me an-y-way.

It's fun-ny how some dis-tance makes ev-'ry-thing seem small; and the fears that once con-trolled me can't get to me at all.

It's time to see what I can do,

ground. My soul __ is spi - ral - ing in

fro - zen frac - tals all a - round. __ And one __ thought

crys - tal - liz - es like an i - cy blast:

f I'm nev - er go - ing back; __ the past is in __ the past! __ *cresc.*

mf

Let it go, __ *ff* let it go, __ and I'll rise __

152

like the break of dawn. Let it go, let it go;

that per-fect girl is gone. Here I stand

in the light of day; let the storm rage on.

The cold nev-er both-ered me an-y-way.

mp   *p*

Linus and Lucy

By Vince Guaraldi
Arranged by Mona Rejino

Moderately fast (♩ =144)

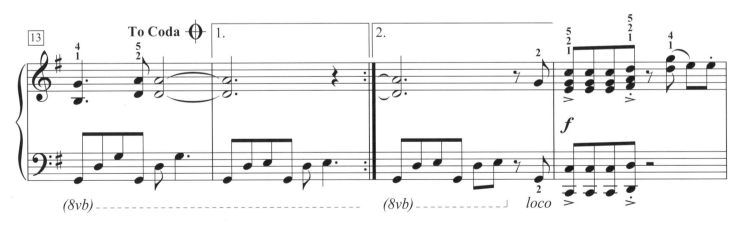

D.S. al Coda

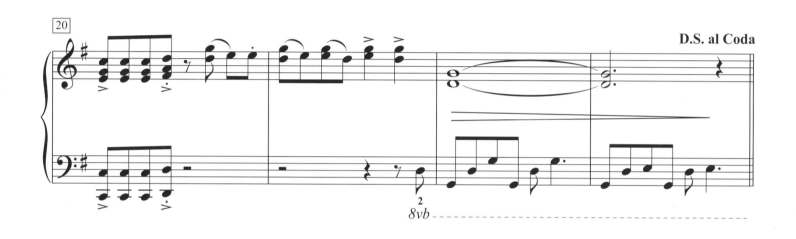

CODA

155

Rolling in the Deep

Words and Music by Adele Adkins
and Paul Epworth
Arranged by Jennifer & Mike Watts

Soul groove (♩ = 108)

With pedal

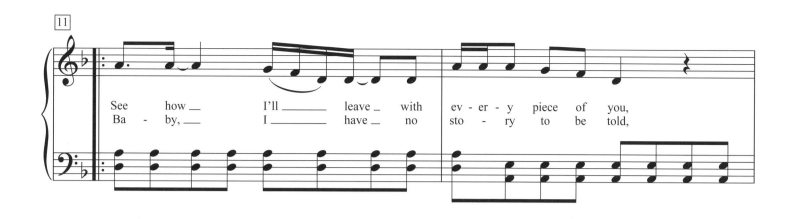

See how ___ I'll _____ leave ___ with ev - er - y piece of you,
Ba - by, ___ I _____ have ___ no sto - ry to be told,

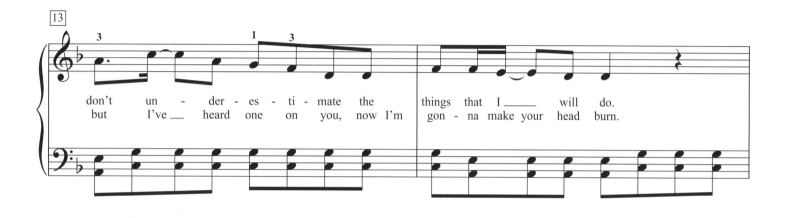

don't un - der - es - ti - mate the things that I ___ will do.
but I've ___ heard one on you, now I'm gon - na make your head burn.

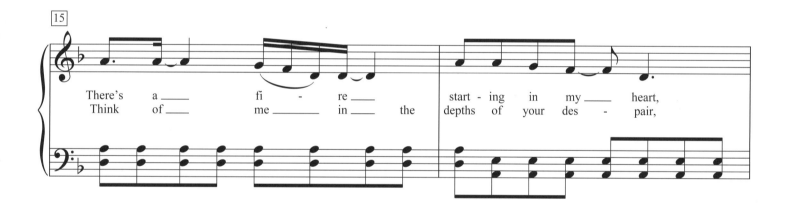

There's a ___ fi - re ___ the start - ing in my ___ heart,
Think of ___ me _____ in ___ the depths of your des - pair,

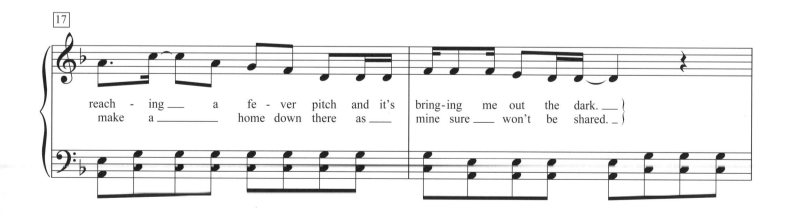

reach - ing ___ a fe - ver pitch and it's bring-ing me out the dark. ___
make a _____ home down there as ___ mine sure ___ won't be shared. _

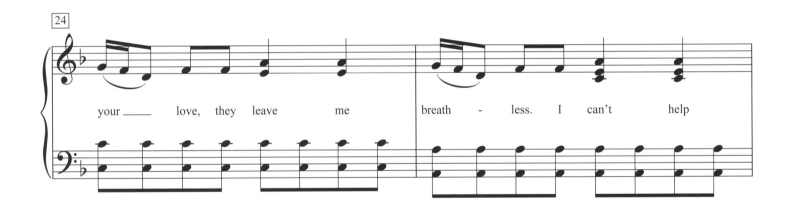

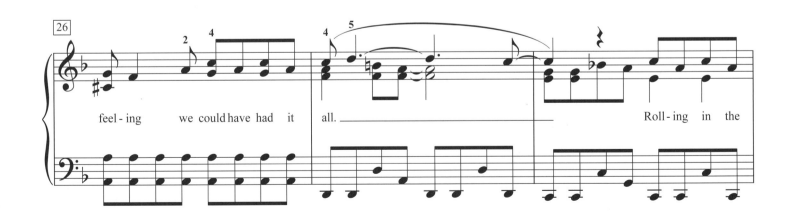

deep. _____ You had my heart in - side _____ of your hand, _

____ and you played ___ it ___ to the beat. _____

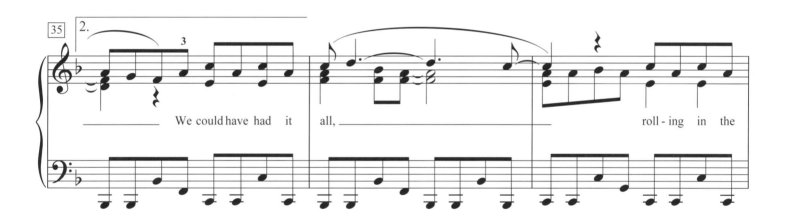

_____ We could have had it all, _____ roll - ing in the

deep. _____ You had my heart in - side _____ of your hand _

159

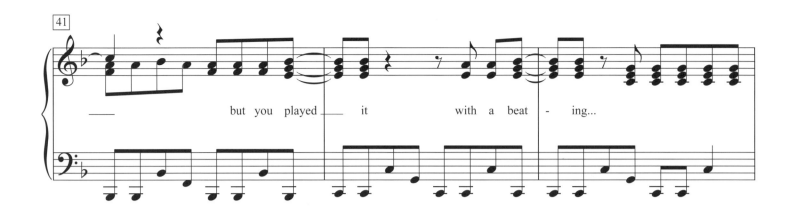

but you played ___ it with a beat \- ing...

Throw your __ soul __through ev \- er \- y o \- pen door, count your __ bless \- ings to

find what you look for. Turn my sor \- rows in \- to treas \-ured gold. You'll

pay me ___ back in kind and reap just what you could have had it

all. _____ Roll-ing in the deep. _____

_____ You had my heart in - side _____ of your hand, _

_____ and you played ___ it to the beat. _____ We could have had it

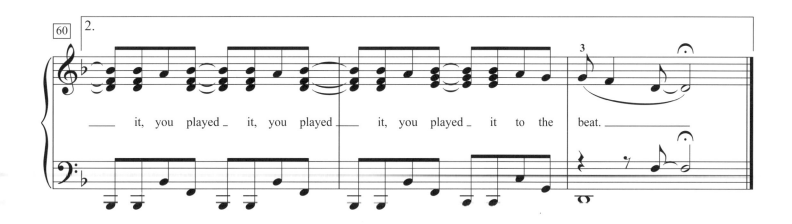

_____ it, you played _ it, you played ___ it, you played _ it to the beat. _____

161

Scales and Arpeggios

from THE ARISTOCATS

Words and Music by Richard M. Sherman
and Robert B. Sherman
Arranged by Mona Rejino

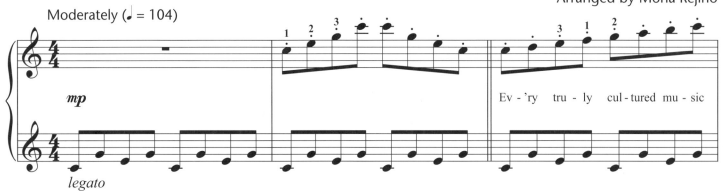

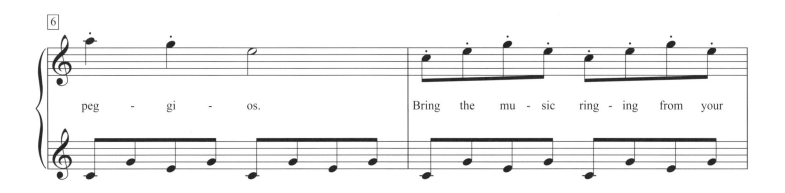

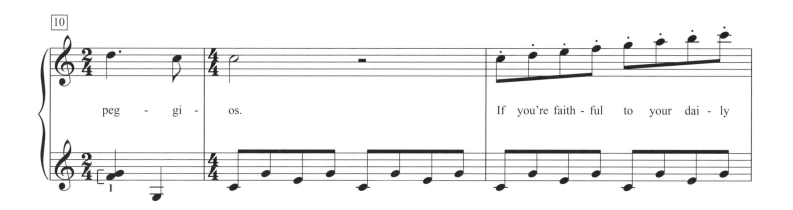

peg - gi - os. If you're faith - ful to your dai - ly

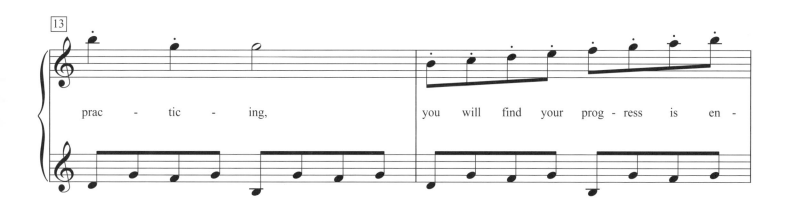

prac - tic - ing, you will find your prog - ress is en -

cour - ag - ing. Do mi so mi do mi so mi fa la so it goes,

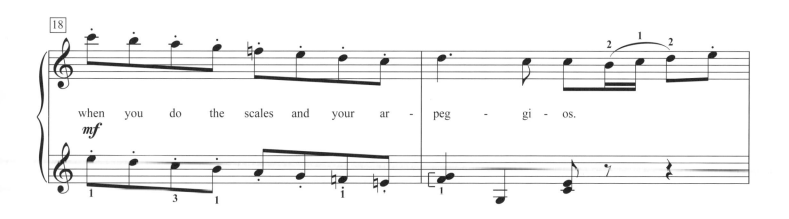

when you do the scales and your ar - peg - gi - os.

mf

Do mi so do, do so mi do. Do mi so do, do so mi do.

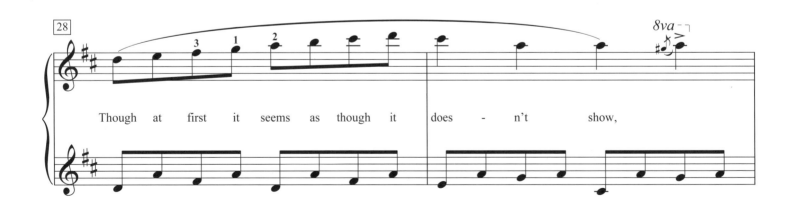

Though at first it seems as though it does - n't show,

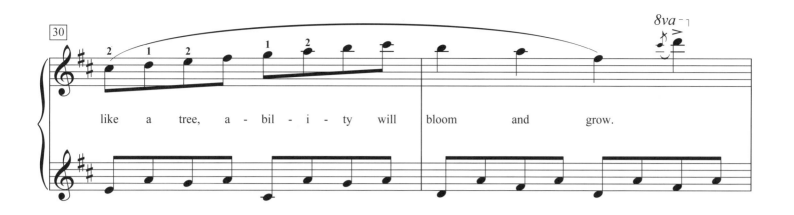

like a tree, a-bil-i-ty will bloom and grow.

If you're smart you'll learn by heart what ev - 'ry art - ist knows:
rall.

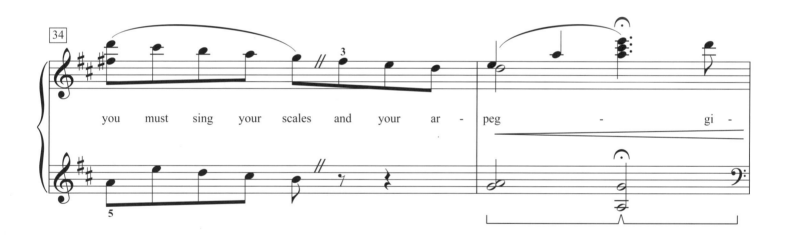

you must sing your scales and your ar - peg - gi -

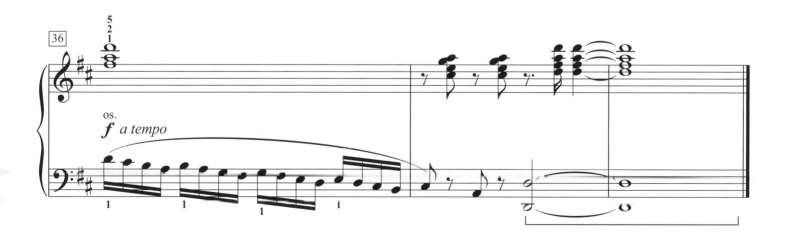

os.
f a tempo

Someone Like You

Words and Music by Adele Adkins
and Dan Wilson
Arranged by Mona Rejino

Piano Ballad (♩ = 69)

With pedal

hate to turn up ___ out of the blue un-in-vit-ed, but I ___ could-n't stay a-way, ___ I could-n't fight it. I had

hoped you'd see my face ___ and that you'd be re-mind-ed that, for me, ___ it is-n't o - ver.

Nev - er mind, ___ I'll ___ find ___ some-one like

you. ___ I wish noth-ing but the best ___ for ___ you, ___

too. Don't for - get me, I beg. ___ I ___ re -

Nothing compares, no worries or cares, regrets and mistakes, they're memories made.

mp

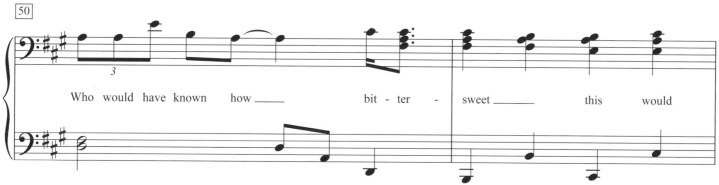

Who would have known how ____ bittersweet ____ this would

taste? *rit.* Never mind, I'll __ find __ someone like ____

mp *a tempo*

____ you. ____ I wish nothing but __ the best __ for __ you. __

____ Don't forget me, I beg. __ I re-

f

member you said, ____ "Some-times it lasts in love, but some-times it hurts in-

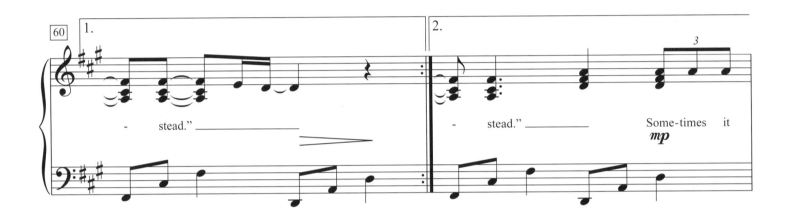

1. -stead." ____

2. -stead." ____ Some-times it

mp

lasts in love, but some-times it hurts in -stead. ____

rit.

172

The Sound of Music

from THE SOUND OF MUSIC

Lyrics by Oscar Hammerstein II
Music by Richard Rodgers
Arranged by Fred Kern

Tenderly, with expression (♩ = 96)

mu - sic. My heart wants to sing ev - 'ry song it

hears. My heart wants to beat like the wings of the birds that rise from the

lake to the trees. My heart wants to sing like a chime that flies from a

church on a breeze, to laugh like a brook when it trips and falls o - ver

Take Five

By Paul Desmond
Arranged by Mona Rejino

Moderately fast (♩ =144)

178

A Thousand Miles

Words and Music by Vanessa Carlton
Arranged by Mona Rejino

True Colors

Words and Music by Billy Steinberg
and Tom Kelly
Arranged by Jennifer Linn

Relaxed (♩ = 80)

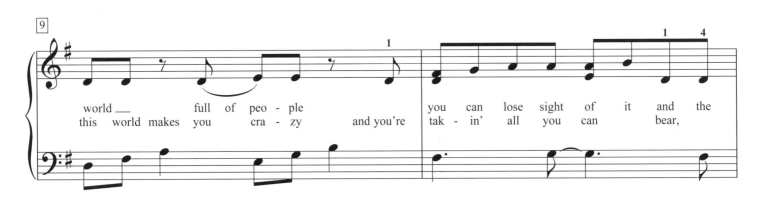